PANIC BEHAVIOR

Discussion and Readings

*Studies
in Psychology*

Consulting Editors:

L. JOSEPH STONE
AND DWIGHT W. CHAPMAN
Vassar College

PANIC BEHAVIOR

Discussion and Readings

DUANE P. SCHULTZ

Mary Washington College, University of Virginia

RANDOM HOUSE • NEW YORK

SECOND PRINTING

Manufactured in the United States of America by
The Colonial Press Inc., Clinton, Massachusetts

ACKNOWLEDGMENTS

The author wishes to acknowledge the assistance of the administration and library staff of Mary Washington College, University of Virginia. Appreciation is also expressed to the authors of the articles reprinted for their permission and helpful suggestions, and to my wife for her insightful criticisms and patience.

Contents

PANIC BEHAVIOR

Discussion and Readings

I

Introduction: The Problem and Nature of Panic

THE PROBLEM OF PANIC

The problem of panic behavior has long been of practical and theoretical significance. Panic has contributed to a needlessly high loss of life not only in both natural and man-made disaster situations, but also in the military, where troops engaged in panic flight in the face of the enemy have, at times, opened the way to tactical, and in some cases, strategic defeats.

From a theoretical standpoint, knowledge of the conditions and causes of panic behavior is necessary in order to provide a thorough and systematic framework within which to more fully understand and predict crowd or group behavior. Indeed, until we are able to anticipate those conditions—internal and/or external to the group—which can cause the group to no longer function, or even to exist as a group, our understanding of such behavior will remain incomplete.

Since the advent of nuclear weaponry and sophisticated delivery devices, the problem of panic has become more intensely critical. We are now faced with the possibility of the greatest disaster threat of all times—a nuclear holocaust. We are warned by some writers that if a nuclear war were unleashed there would be mass panic behavior on a nationwide level which would cause more chaos and social disorganization than the effects of the bombs themselves.

Yet while our knowledge of other aspects of group behavior has increased significantly in the past two decades, our knowledge of panic behavior has shown very little substantive increase since LaPiere's intuitive analysis of the problem in 1938. As noted by Quarantelli (1954)* and Schultz (1964a, 1964b), most of the literature on panic consists of *post hoc* impressionistic speculations with little substantive material amenable to systematic interpretation. Thus in the entire literature relating to the nonadaptive behavior of panic, there have been only two empirical investigations of the problem: J. R. P. French, Jr. (1944), and Alexander Mintz (1951). Other aspects of social psychology have generated an ever-increasing body of experimental research, but the problem of panic has been virtually avoided. To be sure, some other aspects of group behavior permit of more rigid and precise control and experimentation than does the social phenomenon of panic, which indeed, some would say is "impossible" to produce, control, and study in the laboratory situation. Nevertheless, the fact of the difficulty of its treatment by our traditional tools and techniques of research should not diminish its importance. As Robert I. Watson has noted, "It has been

* For full bibliographic data on works cited throughout these introductions and discussions, see the Bibliography at the end of the book. The notes and references originally accompanying the individual articles are printed along with the articles.

said that some psychologists, even in our own day, become too enamored of mathematics leading to a state of affairs where if a problem was quantifiable, no matter how trivial, it was scientific, while an important problem if non-quantifiable would be disdained." *

In this connection, the purpose of this book is hopefully heuristic in nature. All of the theories of panic behavior will be presented, discussed, and evaluated in terms of their points of agreement and points of difference. The two empirical investigations of panic, plus several other articles of interest in the area, will be presented, and the last section will deal with the possibility of a panic in a nationwide nuclear attack.

Should this discussion serve to stimulate and direct theoretical and research efforts in this all-important area of social behavior, it will have served its purpose. To this end, the book is dedicated.

THE NATURE OF PANIC

That the literature on panic is characterized by many ambiguities, tenuous generalizations, and sensationalistic news reports, is attested to by the many and varied definitions of the word itself and by the word's misuse in our everyday speech. In newspaper accounts of fires, ship collisions, earthquakes, and the like, the word panic is constantly used to denote what may in actuality be simple flight behavior which, in many cases, is the only rational way to respond to such disasters. Ordinarily, people do not prefer to stay in a collapsing or burning building any more than they prefer to remain in the path of a speeding automobile—the point being that flight, per se, is not an automatic indicator of panic behavior. Examples of other uses of this term include reference to downswings in the economy of a

---

* *The Great Psychologists.* Philadelphia: Lippincott, 1963, pp. 206-207.

country, or simple apprehension of an approaching event. Not uncommon, for example is the college student's complaint, "I'm panicked about this exam!"

In view of this confusion regarding the word itself, we must first attempt an operational definition of the concept with which we are concerned before going on to discuss theoretical issues.

Paul Foreman (1953) has suggested that there are two conceptions of panic prevalent in the sociological and psychological literature. One conception, as represented by Hadley Cantril (1943) and Irving Janis (1951), emphasizes the covert emotional state of a terrorized individual; a person who is distraught and demoralized and in an intense state of fear. Panic, according to this view, is primarily an internal state which may or may not lead to overt flight behavior.

The second conception of panic, as represented by Enrico Quarantelli (1954), considers flight behavior as a necessary condition. Quarantelli defines panic behavior as, "an acute fear reaction marked by a loss of self-control which is followed by nonsocial and nonrational flight behavior" (1954, p. 272).

Thus in the first case, a group can be labeled as "panicking" if its members are intensely fearful *without* engaging in flight behavior whereas in the second this label can only be properly applied if the group does engage in flight behavior.

For the purpose of providing a unifying framework within which to discuss panic behavior, we shall consider overt flight behavior as necessary to a definition of panic, adding the following two considerations:

(1) That flight behavior must lead to the destruction of the group, as a psychological group.

(2) That flight behavior must be nonadaptive for the physical survival of the group members.

The second condition follows from the first and both imply a loss of consideration for one's fellows.

Several reasons are operative in our deciding on this particular definition of panic, one of which being that the first definition discussed above stresses intense fear which is not necessarily manifested overtly. Yet surely there are many instances where the individual members of a group experience an intense degree of fear and yet are still able to respond rationally in a manner adaptive to the situation. There have been theater or auditorium fires, for example, in which people have filed out through exits in an orderly manner incurring no injury or loss of life. Those concerned may have experienced varying degrees of fear, but we certainly could not consider their behavior as panic. Similarly, the fact a group engages in flight behavior is not, in and of itself, sufficient to describe that group as being in a state of panic. During the atomic bombing of Hiroshima flight behavior was widespread as people fled the city in a high state of fear. Yet Janis (1951) considers this flight behavior to have been an adaptive response; those who did not flee were killed by the rapid spread of fire. Similarly, Quarantelli (1960) notes, in the study of localized disasters in America, flight behavior which was adaptive to the situation at hand and could not, therefore, be called panic behavior.

How can we distinguish between flight behavior in one situation as being an adaptive response while in another, as, for example, a theater fire, it is viewed as an example of panic and entirely nonadaptive? Perhaps this can best be answered by saying that panic is, in part, situationally determined by the number of escape routes that the situation provides. Given the necessary conditions of fear and flight, that which determines the adaptive or nonadaptive character of the flight is the degree to which escape can be successfully effected. Janis, Chapman, Gillin, and Spiegel (1955) address themselves to this point in their article presented in Chapter VI. Given blocked or in some way limited numbers of exits or escape routes, the potentially adaptive character of flight gives way to nonadaptive behavior in which people quickly clog or jam the few escape routes so as to render them, in effect, closed, leaving an even smaller number of such routes.

When such a situation occurs, we are faced with a clear-cut instance of panic behavior: a fear-induced flight which further limits an already small number of escape routes, and in which the fear and terror become self-perpetuating. The three essential components of our definition of panic thus become fear, flight, and limited access to escape routes. In a large-scale disaster of the magnitude of the atomic bombings, however, flight behavior is not generally limited by a small number of escape routes and hence is a realistic resolution of the crisis situation. It is significant to note that Janis's report (1951) revealed only one clear-cut instance of panic behavior during the Hiroshima attack: a restricted environment on the banks of a river where the crowd was pressing closer and closer to the water in order to escape the searing heat of the flames behind them. As the only direction in which escape was seen possible was towards the water, a number of people closest to the river were pushed in and drowned.

To clarify further our conception of panic, the following two accounts are presented: The Iroquois Theater Fire of 1903, and The Coconut Grove Fire of 1942, both of which testify to the nonadaptive behavior of the participants.

In the Iroquois Theater Fire of 1903:

. . . Somebody had of course yelled 'Fire!'—there is almost always a fool of that species in an audience; and there are always hundreds of people who go crazy the moment they hear the word. . . .

The horror in the auditorium was beyond all description. There were thirty exits, but few of them were marked by lights; some had heavy portieres over the doors, and some of the doors were locked or fastened with levers which no one knew how to work.

It was said that some of the exit doors . . . were either rusted or frozen. They were finally burst open, but precious moments had been lost—moments which meant death for many behind those doors. The fire-escape ladders could not accommodate the crowd, and many fell or jumped to death on the pavement below. Some were not killed only because they landed on the cushion of bodies of those who had gone before.

But it was inside the house that the greatest loss of life occurred, especially on the stairways leading down from the second balcony. Here most of the dead were trampled or smothered, though many jumped or fell over the balustrade to the floor of the foyer. In places on the stairways, particularly where a turn caused a jam, bodies were piled seven or eight feet deep. . . . An occasional living person was found in the heaps, but most of these were terribly injured. The heel prints on the dead faces mutely testified to the cruel fact that human animals stricken by terror are as mad and ruthless as stampeding cattle. Many bodies had the clothes torn from them, and some had the flesh trodden from their bones (E. Foy and A. F. Harlow, *Clowning Through Life*. New York: Dutton, 1928, pp. 104-113).

Never before had such a disaster occurred so quickly.

In just eight minutes, from the start of the fire until all lay dead, injured, or had escaped, more than 500 people perished.

Ironically, the theater itself did *not* burn; performances could have been given in it a few days afterward since little more than the upholstery on the seats was destroyed.

In the Coconut Grove Fire of 1942:

> Every available table was taken. . . . a girl, her hair ablaze, hurtled across the floor screaming "Fire!"
>
> That shriek heralded catastrophe. Some 800 guests, insane with panic, lunged in a wild scramble to get out the only way they knew—the revolving-door exit. Flames flashed with incredible swiftness. . . . Smoke swirled in choking masses through hallways. The revolving doors jammed as the terror-stricken mob pushed them in both directions at the same time. Blazing draperies fell, setting women's evening gowns and hair on fire. Patrons were hurled under tables and trampled to death. Others tripped and choked the 6-foot-wide stairway up from the Melody Lounge. Those behind swarmed over them and piled up in layers—layers of corpses. . . .
>
> The fire was quickly brought under control, but the fatal damage was done (*Newsweek,* December 7, 1942, pp. 43-44).

Of the 800 patrons, only 100 escaped unhurt, and half of these were employees who were familiar with alternative exits. Approximately 500 persons were killed, making it the second greatest disaster of its kind (the first being the Iroquois Theater Fire). In both cases the fire itself was brought quickly under control. It was the nonadaptive behavior which caused the majority of the deaths.

Thus far, our discussion of the nature of panic has

been limited to unorganized groups, such as theater audiences and ship passengers. There is yet another type of panic that must be considered: panic in organized groups. It has been suggested by Brown (1954) and Schultz (1964b) that no discussion of panic behavior can be complete without a consideration of the organizational structure of the group, that is whether the group is organized or unorganized. Observations of one type of group will not necessarily apply to the other. McDougall (1920) suggests that organized groups are characterized by (1) a continuity of existence, (2) an awareness of membership, (3) interaction with other organizations, and (4) differentiation of functions—the traditional example of such a group being a military unit, some of which have been known to engage in panic flight to the rear. The difference in the environmental situation between a military unit in combat and an unorganized group necessitates a modification of our panic definition. A military unit in flight is not usually restricted to a limited number of escape routes. True, they can go in only one direction, but beyond this, they are not limited in their escape routes as is a theater audience. Yet from the standpoint of their survival (and that of neighboring units), the panic flight of soldiers can be equally nonadaptive. If they remain together as a unit they might fight a strategic withdrawal reaction and so regroup at a later time and place still intact as a unit, although some individuals may have been lost. By dropping their arms and fleeing, however, they cease to exist as a functional unit, a lapse which can result in the loss of the entire battle or campaign and the subsequent death or capture of a large number of them. The causes of military panics will be discussed in Chapter III.

As an example of military panic, the following is cited:

> As the regiment was trotting back in marching column on the road, the regimental commander sent an aide to the head of the column to bring it to a walk. As this officer was galloping along from the direction of the enemy, his pace was regarded as a sign of the seriousness of the situation. When the officers tried to gain the heads of their troops by galloping, the troopers followed suit and soon the entire regiment was galloping away from the enemy, and overran a Prussian battery. Only after miles and some casualties was it possible to bring the regiment to a halt (Von Altrock, 1930, p. 116).

Thus in both organized and unorganized groups, panic behavior expresses itself in flight, "which results in increasing the danger for the self and for others rather than in reducing it" (Janis, *et al.*, 1955, p. 1).

In our evaluation of the various theories of panic behavior, this distinction between organized and unorganized groups will be considered, Chapter II relating to unorganized groups, and Chapter III discussing organized groups.

II

Panic in Unorganized Groups

DISCUSSION

EARLY THEORIES OF PANIC— McDOUGALL, LaPIERE, CANTRIL, MINTZ

The first theorist to discuss the problem of panic in unorganized groups was William McDougall in his book, *The Group Mind* (1920). For McDougall, panic is the crudest and simplest manifestation of collective mental life, the "collective intensification of the instinctive excitement," with its emotion of fear and its impulse to flight" (1920, p. 36). This collective intensification is induced by emotional contagion or "primitive sympathy." The instinctive excitement and fear is brought on by the perception of danger and spread from one or a few members of a group to the entire group by emotional contagion. As each individual perceives the overt symptoms of fear of his fellows, "his own impulse and his own emotion rise to a higher pitch of intensity, and their expressions become correspondingly accentuated. . . . So the expressions of each member of the crowd work upon all other members within sight and hearing of him to intensify their excitement" (1920, p. 36). And thus ensues a vicious cycle of intense emotion begetting more intense emotion, until all members of the crowd are in the highest possible emotional state. Thus, according to McDougall, a large group of people may engage in panic behavior in reaction to a threat which may be perceptible to only a small portion of the group's membership.

In *Collective Behavior* (1938), Richard LaPiere views the problem of panic behavior as a collective solution to the sudden adjustment problem which is created by the perception and definition of a crisis. He notes that two conditions or circumstances are necessary for the occurrence of panic: (1) the definition of the crisis situation, and (2) the lack of regimental behavior and/or leadership to cope with the crisis. The individual members of the crowd, then, must be aware of actually present danger or believe that danger is present.

To LaPiere, the immediate antecedents of panic are individual, not collective. When a crisis situation has occurred and been defined, social interaction is interrupted and the situation is, at least momentarily, reduced to an aggregate of shocked individuals. At such time all action is suspended, and the members of the situation behave as isolated individuals, each trying to find an adequate response to the crisis.

A group of reacting individuals in a theater, or auditorium, or on a ship, cannot long refrain from interacting since their individual reactions are likely to bring them into physical contact with one another.

Therefore, LaPiere feels, it is inevitable that this period of individual behavior will be very brief and will be followed by some form of collective behavior. And unless some form of leadership or regimental behavior intervenes, this collective behavior will take the form of panic.

While the members of the group are individually fumbling for a mode of adjustment, each is attempting to respond to the stimuli which were defined as a crisis. Should some one individual cry "Fire!" or "Help!" or simply scream, the members of the group may then be led to respond again to stimuli of social origin—i.e., to direct their attention to the source of the cry. The cry itself is but the fumbling effort of one member of the group to adjust to the crisis. It is individual, purposeless action which is comparable to other random actions. Unlike other random actions, however, the cry has the potentiality for invoking attention and, thus, response from others.

With the attention of his fellows focused on him, the one who cried may become the leader of the situation. He does not lead the other members of the situation in the sense that a lecturer leads an audience or an officer leads his soldiers. On the basis of the nonvocal actions which accompany his cry, he leads those who have been attracted by his cry only to the extent of providing them with a pattern of action which they can mimic.

Panic interaction is a direct consequence of the mimicry by many panic-stricken individuals of the overt behavior of some one of them (1938, p. 447).

Thus, mimicry is introduced by LaPiere to explain the transition from individual to group behavior. From this description it would seem that, to LaPiere, it is this spontaneous leadership which, through mimicry, determines the type and direction of the group's behavior. He is careful to note that the spontaneous leadership offered may be positive and constructive as well as negative and destructive. And he also notes that many potential panic situations are averted when a "synchronizing leadership" emerges which coordinates the patterns of behavior in a constructive way, providing for behavior which is adaptive to the situation. Thus, the appearance and definition of a crisis situation need not always result in panic behavior; a crisis is a necessary, but not a sufficient, condition for panic to occur.

Hadley Cantril, in his 1940 analysis of the American reaction to Orson Welles' *The Invasion from Mars* broadcast, also discusses panic in unorganized groups. But it is questionable whether the flight reaction of people to this broadcast can be considered as panic in the sense it was defined in Chapter I. Indeed, it appears to be questionable whether in this case there actually was much flight behavior of any kind (Quarantelli, 1960).

The point of interest in Cantril's analysis for our purposes is that not everyone who was exposed to the "threat" did attempt to flee. Some of the participants who unequivocally accepted the crisis without seeking any further verification did flee, while those others who did seek information and corroboration did not. In considering this aspect of the incident, Cantril posits the existence of certain background factors which would render some individuals more susceptible to panic terror than others. He discusses these factors in terms of lack of critical ability, or suggestibility.

As to the cause of panic, Cantril invokes the perception of crisis or danger of an overwhelming magnitude. Panic will occur, he notes, when a highly cherished value is threatened and when no reduction or elimination of the threat is apparent. Cantril describes panic behavior as being nondirectional and useless in attempting to cope with the crisis. The Martian invasion, as described by the broadcast, was not a situation in which the individual could preserve one value by sacrificing another; it was a situation in which he stood to lose all of his values at once and nothing could be done to save any of them. Panic was inescapable.

Alexander Mintz's article, "Non-Adaptive Group Behavior" (1951), is reprinted in Chapter V as an example of the only systematic experimental investigation of panic behavior. However, in order to completely cover those theories dealing with panic in unorganized groups, it is necessary to present briefly his main theoretical points in this chapter.

Mintz takes issue with other panic theorists who propose that intense emotion is essential to panic behavior, suggesting, rather, that panic is a function of the perceived reward structure of the situation. As he sees it, nonadaptive behavior arises from a breakdown in cooperation, which then causes the flight to appear to be adaptive from the point of view of the individual.

> Cooperative behavior is required for the common good but has very different consequences for the individual depending on the behavior of others. Thus at a theater fire, if everyone leaves in an orderly manner, everybody is safe, and an individual waiting for his turn is not sacrificing his interests. But, if the cooperative pattern of behavior is disturbed, the usual advice, "Keep your head, don't push, wait for your turn, and you will be safe," ceases to be valid. If the exits are blocked, the person following this advice is likely to be

burned to death. In other words, if everybody cooperates, there is no conflict between the needs of the individual and those of the group. However, the situation
changes completely as soon as a minority of people
cease to cooperate. A conflict between the needs of the
group and the selfish needs of the individual then arises.
An individual who recognizes this state of things and
who wants to benefit the group must sacrifice his own
selfish needs (p. 151).

To complete our discussion of panic in unorganized
groups, articles by Paul Foreman and Enrico Quarantelli are presented.

Foreman's article is not clearly defined as pertaining to either organized or unorganized groups. However, one of the causal conditions for panic which he
proposes is the absence of prepared or conventionalized behavior to deal with the crisis situation. And
since the presence of such behavior is characteristic of
organized military groups, his article will be discussed
in this chapter. Certain of his formulations, however,
are also appropriate for panic in the military and will
be discussed in Chapter III.

Following these two articles, some over-all points
of agreement and disagreement among the theories
of panic in unorganized groups will be discussed.

PANIC THEORY
Paul B. Foreman

At least three ideas of panic are current in American
social science literature. The quite standard economic

Reprinted from *Sociology and Social Research*, 1953, **37**, 295-304, by
permission of the publisher and the author.

interpretation holds panic to be a mass response to a market collapse, real or imagined, the purpose of which is to escape capital loss after a period of inflation or overtrading. In sociological and social-psychological literature two somewhat less clearly established conceptions appear. In the first of these, as in the writing of Cantril, Janis, Meerloo, and Sullivan,[1] panic refers either to the feelings or the overt behavior of a terrorized individual—a person utterly demoralized or distraught and then gripped by an intense state of fear and anxiety. Presumably, fear and anxiety are cued by the perception of a great, unanticipated and seemingly unmanageable crisis, and, among other possible reactions, may lead to pell-mell flight. According to the second usage, one also common in historical writing, panic is construed as a type of rout, a very ephemeral form of collective behavior occurring in face-to-face contact groups or through mediated communication in masses. Among better-known sources, this construction has appeared in the work of Lanham, LaPiere, and Reuter and Hart.[2]

The contrast between these two latter conceptions of panic has been sharpened by Janis' recent review of World War II air raid reactions.[3] Accepting the idea of panic as a terror state and as "nonadaptive" personal behavior in response to a crisis, Janis did not

[1] Hadley Cantril and others, *The Invasion from Mars* (Princeton: Princeton University Press, 1940); Hadley Cantril, "Causes and Control of Riot and Panic," *Public Opinion Quarterly*, 7:669-79, 1943; Irving L. Janis, *Air War and Emotional Stress* (New York: McGraw-Hill Book Company, Inc., 1951); Harry Stack Sullivan, "Psychiatric Aspects of Morale," *American Journal of Sociology*, 47:277-301, 1941.
[2] C. T. Lanham, "Panic" in Joseph I. Greene, *The Infantry Journal Reader* (Garden City: Doubleday, Doran and Company, Inc., 1943); R. T. LaPiere, *Collective Behavior* (New York: McGraw-Hill Book Company, Inc., 1938); E. B. Reuter and C. W. Hart, *Introduction to Sociology* (New York: McGraw-Hill Book Company, Inc., 1933).
[3] Janis, *op. cit.*, esp. pp. 1-66 on reactions to atomic blasts at Hiroshima and Nagasaki.

pause to contrast his views with panic conceived as
rout. Rather, he dismissed the latter as an *"a priori,
stereotyped conception of mass panic."* [4] He was
strongly inclined to discount panic references in earlier
studies of reactions at Hiroshima and Nagasaki—
studies which, as he held, treated panic casually but
almost invariably, it would seem, in the sense of rout.
Janis' views can be epitomized by the following ex-
cerpts:

> The above assertions (from earlier reviews) sound like
> authoritative, well-established propositions, *as though
> the panic were in the same category as the fact that
> there was a mass exodus from the burning cities* . . .
> In the absence of precise, detailed observations of
> escape behavior, one cannot make an adequate evalu-
> ation of the degree of emotional control exhibited by
> the survivors. To stop and to attempt to extricate others
> in the face of a rapidly spreading conflagration would
> sometimes be tantamount to futile sacrifice of one's own
> life. We cannot be sure, therefore, that those who fled
> without stopping to help others were behaving im-
> pulsively, since we cannot exclude the possibility that
> they may have been acting on the basis of a realistic
> appraisal of a danger situation. Our information is too
> incomplete to permit any fine judgments to be made;
> from what little is available, it would be unwarranted
> to conclude that there was a sizeable frequency of in-
> appropriate, negligent, or asocial behavior merely be-
> cause some instances of abandonment have been re-
> ported.[5] [Italics added]

Janis sought to distill inferences from World War II
bombing situations which might be pertinent for the
planning of postdisaster controls. Knowledge about

---

[4] *Ibid.*, p. 27.
[5] *Ibid.*, pp. 30, 37. See also his "Typical Disaster Experience," pp. 6-7,
a case study which discloses flight to the Hiroshima hinterland but
highlights only personal terror.

human stampedes might be as meaningful for this interest as knowledge about the "inappropriate, negligent, or asocial" behavior which Janis identified as panic. It can be quickly demonstrated that ideas of panic as a terror state or as the overt behavior of a distraught individual and the idea of panic as rout can induce confusion. It would be consistent with Janis' premises to pay particular attention in the aftermath at Hiroshima to excited individuals huddling in the ruined city; it would be consistent with the view that panic is rout to examine the behavior of survivors fleeing toward the Hiroshima hinterlands. It is logical for Janis to hold, as he has done, that panic rarely occurs unless immediate physical danger is overwhelming *and no apparent avenues of escape exist.*[6] It would be equally logical for those holding panic to be a form of rout to conclude from the accounts of the *General Slocum* fire, for example, that panic occurs in the presence of events interpreted as acutely and uncontrollably dangerous *only when avenues of possible escape are evident.*[7]

Assuming the conception of panic as rout and holding the idea that knowledge about this behavior might be valuable in military operations as well as for post-disaster control of civilian populations, this paper reports the findings of an attempt to apply case study techniques for comparative analysis of a series of historical incidents in order to codify theory and to develop an initial series of propositions on panic control. Twenty-nine incidents were reviewed in detail; twenty-five other cases for which less complete information could be found were also considered. Unfortunately, no data from World War II or Korean inci-

---

[6] *Ibid.*, pp. 40, 193.
[7] *New York Times*, June 16, 1904, ff.

dents are included. If this approach is suggestive, a review of classified documents concerning such cases should permit extensive revision or supplement to the theory developed by the present effort.

One of the most persistent problems faced in this review of panic incidents has been the need for distinguishing succinctly between antecedent and predisposing conditions on one hand and cause on the other. References to either in the literature are frequently little more than rationalizations elaborated by hindsight imputation. By superimposing the data of case on case, however, it is possible to clarify theory at this point and to suggest that background conditions become factors in panic only as reactions to a crisis stimulus are shaped by them. In the few available accounts of mass panics, that is, stampedes induced in dispersed populations by some form of mediated communication,[8] the stimulus leading to rout clearly linked antecedent tensions with immediate shock. This was a major force in the hoax news broadcast in Paris on the day of the Bikini test. However, some stampedes in direct contact military groups—for example, in the routs at Chickamauga, Missionary Ridge, Gumbinnen, and Tannenburg—appear to be almost totally explicable in terms of the quick sequence of events following shock in the course of battle.

As cases were reviewed for this summary, a check was made on all conditions, prior to the shock stimulus, which were presumed to influence rout. They ran a long and dissonant gamut. However, all these conditions can be quickly, if roughly, grouped into types: conditions such as acute fatigue which weaken indi-

---

[8] Louis Wirth, "Consensus and Mass Communication," *American Sociological Review*, 13:1-15, 1948.

iduals organically, those like worry about lack of
nformation concerning expected attacks in war which
create acute emotional tensions and anxiety, those like
novice or stranger status which prevent or impoverish
elf-satisfying group identifications, and those like
awareness of such weapons as guided missiles and
napalm which incite chronic social unrest.[9]

Cause in most panics develops through the linkage
of a shock stimulus and four phases of human reaction
o this stimulus. The stimulus interrupts antecedent
behavior and, frequently it appears, suspends action.
To lead toward panic this stimulus must have sufficient duration, sequence, or repetition to command
ontinued focused attention and to compound terror
responses. Shock or the perception of the crisis as
startling and crisis provoking is the initial reaction to
his stimulus. In situations culminating in panic, shock
s quickly followed by confusion, that is, by individual
nd random efforts to interpret events in terms of
easonable experiences or relatable antecedent situa-
ions. To borrow a phrase from J. T. MacCurdy, shock
nd confusion are phases of "indecisive inactivity oc-
asioned by an emergency." [10] Where interpretations
f the stimulus are so acutely pressing that instanta-
eous action is demanded, the sensing of this acute-
ess frequently blocks logical definition of the crisis
nd induces terror. Initial terror responses include
houts, screams, and excited physical movements. This
s not a lull phase; it is a period of din. These indecisive
cts of initial terror, if not immediately controlled by

A very similar typing, one which does not however distinguish back-
ound conditions and cause, appears in Anselm L. Strauss, "The Lit-
ature on Panic," *Journal of Abnormal and Social Psychology*, 39:317-
3, 1944.

J. T. MacCurdy, *The Structure of Morale* (New York: The Mac-
illan Company, 1944).

an overwhelming order-producing stimulus, compoun
into bedlam. Such reactions may be significant at firs
as releases for overwhelming tension; quickly, how
ever, they serve as reinforcing stimuli for the terror c
others and may be reflected back, circularwise, to re
inforce the frenzy of the original actor. Linked i
these ways, the terror of interacting individuals :
heightened. Occasionally, participant observers recor
the fact that these augmented terror responses serv
to reduce confidence in whatever, if any, organizin
interpretations of the crisis had been effected and t
establish convictions of doom. Terror movement
among whatever else they may suggest, may chann
attention and direct activity to flight. Actors who off
such suggestions are in this context flight models.
Panic is activated when interacting terrorized ind
viduals surge away in flight.

Panic is extremely impulsive action. Frequently it
characterized as individualistic or egocentric actio
This is true in the sense that panic as a design fo
personal survival obeys no custom. The action o
people in rout is, however, given common characte
by at least two things: first, by circular and chain su
gestions presented during flight; second, by the ide

---

[11] No clearer example of model suggestion for flight could be provid
than this: "An American battalion holds a reserve position in a she
torn wood. Enemy artillery has been intermittently strafing the positi
since dusk. The Americans in their foxholes are getting what sle
they can. At 11:00 p.m. the battalion commander, accompanied by l
adjutant, starts an inspection of his lines. A runner dashes up an
hands him a message. The Major reads it. He calls to his adjuta
who is a short distance away, "Come on! Let's beat it!" The two st
to the rear at a dead run. Before they have covered two hundred yar
the entire battalion is in wild flight behind them. It races more th
ten kilometers before it can be stopped. The message to the Maj
had directed him to report to the regimental command post as fast
he could get there. He was complying with the order." Lanham, c
cit., p. 275.

ity or similarity in escape opportunities afforded by
he setting in which rout proceeds.

Milling and canalization of milling responses into
light by effective models continue to appear when
out is in process. Milling is accentuated wherever
light is blocked; flight proceeds when a participant
its upon some newly evident means of escape. If
nany avenues of escape are apparent, the terrorizing
pressure of the perceived crisis is lessened; if few or
no avenues of escape are evident or if available aven-
es are blocked, terror-accentuating pressure is augmented.

The tensions of rout are acute and tend to be short-
ived. People in panic may attain safety; they may
trive until death, strain, fatigue, or despair ends their
participation; or, given sufficient suggestions, they
nay shift to some other form of collective behavior—
perhaps that of a mob or an orgiastic crowd.[12] Panic
n the first battle at Bull Run subsided to the dismal
rek of a defeated, unorganized horde when the acute
pressure of Confederate pursuit was withdrawn.
Chance separations of escaping individuals from the
churning aggregate of a stampede may also lessen
ensions and terminate flight. The usual ending of
panic clearly is not a group process; panic ends as
elective influences eliminate individuals from rout.
But panic behavior is not necessarily complete when
light terminates. There are common sequelae to panic
—fatigue and stupor, extreme anxiety, excitability and

Joseph H. Douglass ("The Funeral of Sister President," *Journal of
Abnormal and Social Psychology*, 44:217-23, 1939) called attention to
ne crowd which did not seem to conform to commonly indicated
rowd types. What Douglass did not consider is that situational re-
efinitions in the period of activity of his considered group may have
one precisely what is suggested above for panic groups, that is, com-
letely changed its type as a collective behavior form.

aggression, perhaps persistent terror and, not infrequently, secondary panics.

This simple theory of panic requires at least two supplements and several specific provisos. The first supplement rests on the experience of survivors at Halifax, Hiroshima, and Nagasaki. It is that as the immediate impact of a devastating stimulus approaches the proportions of absolute incomprehensibility, this impact alone may be sufficient to trigger flight reactions. The second supplement is that if a stimulus, prior to its occurrence, is linguistically defined as unmanageable, its name alone can induce immediate terror and panic. There are accounts indicating that the cry of "Gas!" so operated during World War I. There are accounts indicating that the cry of "Napalm!" may have operated in this way in Korea. It is also reasonable to suppose that the tactics of the Communist Chinese in Korea which call for "human wave" assaults accompanied by the sounding of bugles and other noise are somewhat similarly construed.[13]

The summary theory presented above, as a crude form of natural history derived from but a few cases, needs several specific provisos beyond the patent one that these ideas might be shaken greatly by the introduction of new evidence. First, it does not assume that all individuals interacting in a social situation culminating in panic react in the same way. Perceptions of

---

[13] This point is briefly mentioned in Alfred L. Lindesmith and Anselm L. Strauss, *Social Psychology* (New York: The Dryden Press, 1949) p. 332. These authors go so far as to state, "Human beings usually become panicked in situations which have previously been linguistically defined as fearful or terrifying." While "usually" might be hard to prove, this hypothesis might profitably be examined when more complete testimony is available. Such theory would seem, further, to illuminate many cases of bolting by individuals: the boy who, walking by a graveyard, bolts and runs for his life because he "saw a ghost," is reacting in terms of earlier linguistic interpretations.

a crisis and attempts to orient it certainly do not lead to uniform responses on the part of individuals exposed to a crisis stimulus. Differing antecedent experiences, differing immediate definitions of the crisis stimulus, and such things as differing physical abilities will encourage variable responses. Second, it does not assume that rout develops more or less automatically when certain background factors creating a condition of "panic ripeness" appear. Indeed, it assumes panic usually to be a product of a chain of reactions following a crisis stimulus, and it infers that stampedes do not develop until suggestions for flight are acted upon in a certain way. This is to say that terror does not inevitably breed panic and that, perhaps with very little difference in suggestion, a terror situation might produce a mob or an orgiastic crowd rather than rout.[14] Third, this theory does not assume that panic is "nonadaptive": irrational, inappropriate, negligent, or asocial behavior. Mintz, who has recently published an objection, similar to the position taken here, to the type of panic theory that merely stresses background conditions, mutual facilitation (contagion, suggestion) leading to intense emotional excitement, and regressive behavior, has made this point, although he himself describes panic as "nonadaptive group behavior." Mintz specifies:

---

[14] E. Glover ("Notes on the Psychological Effects of War Conditions on Civilian Populations," *International Journal of Psychoanalysis*, 23: 17-37, 1942) and P. E. Vernon ("Psychological Effects of Air-Raids," *Journal of Abnormal and Social Psychology*, 36:457-76, 1941) confirm the point that terror does not inevitably produce panic. Lindesmith and Strauss (*op. cit.*, p. 497) would include in panic behavior "other than that of physically running away." But this would tend to confuse panic with such distinctive behavior forms as the orgiastic crowd where physical movement and shouting are principally devices of tension release, not acute fear; the mob where action is directed at "getting" some person, group, place, or thing; or the riot where mobs meet or revelers or mobs encounter almost any sharp opposition.

At a theater fire if everyone leaves in an orderly manner everybody is safe and an individual waiting for his turn is not sacrificing his interests. But if the cooperative pattern of behavior is disturbed, the usual advice, "Keep your head, don't push, wait your turn, and you will be safe," ceases to be valid. If the exits are blocked, the person following this advice is likely to be burned to death. In other words, if everybody cooperates there is no conflict between the needs of the individual and those of the group. However, the situation changes completely as soon as a minority of people cease to co-operate . . . People are likely to recognize the threats to themselves and behave accordingly . . . *If a few individuals begin to push, others are apt to recognize that their interests are threatened; they can expect to win their rewards only by pressing their personal advantage at the group's expense.*[15] [Italics added]

The idea that panic is inappropriate, nondiscriminating behavior is age-old. It frequently appears in reviews of military incidents; clearly it has been fostered by the widespread attention given Cantril's *Invasion from Mars*. Cantril wrote of panic as terror produced by suggestibility and assumed that a cardinal purpose of his review was to show people how some individuals reacted unintelligently to the Welles broadcast so that they might avoid or build up resistance to similar hoodwinking.[16] This evaluative premise about panic, no matter if panic is construed as terror or as rout, ignores or underemphasizes the situational redefinitions which recast the significance of action when time is out of joint. Such moralizing appears gross when one recalls the theory behind W. I.

---

[15] Alexander Mintz, "Non-Adaptive Group Behavior," *Journal of Abnormal and Social Psychology*, 46:150-59, 1951.

[16] Cantril and others, *op. cit.*, p. viii. For a review of Cantril's work, see Janis, *op. cit.*, p. 193.

Thomas' dictum: "If men define situations as real, they are real in their consequences." [17]

Perhaps the fact that panic is abhorred is sufficient to explain the almost universal attention given to prevention when its control is considered. Almost nothing has been written about diminution of panic or efforts to quell it once it has been activated, and even less attention has been given to panic incitement or reinforcement. It seems quite possible that obsession with prevention may have retarded panic theory. Quite possibly, panic may be a legitimate device of modern warfare, harsh as this idea may at first seem. Quite possibly, also, attention to control efforts, other than prevention, may result in the improvement of defensive as well as offensive tactics, whether these tactics apply to military or civilian situations. Working from such assumptions, a careful effort was made, when the cases contributing to this review were read, to conceptualize any inference about control, whatever its intent might be. These inferences, not supplemented by free theorizing and cast generally in the form of inducement and reinforcement, can be presented in proposition form, as follows:

1. Although background conditions are not causal factors of panic, deliberate attempts to induce or reinforce terror or panic should succeed more readily where conditions known to be present in prior instances are clearly present and compounded.

2. Where a crisis stimulus provokes a totally incomprehensible disaster, control or selection of background conditions probably has little effect on behavior subsequent to this stimulus.

---

[17] Herbert Blumer, *Critiques of Research in the Social Sciences: I* (New York: Social Science Research Council, 1942), p. 85. See also E. H. Volkart, ed., *Social Behavior and Personality* (New York: Social Science Research Council, 1951), pp. 12-14 *et passim*.

3. For an effective understanding of background conditions weakening individuals organically, producing acute tensions and anxiety, and preventing or impoverishing rewarding group identifications, considerable insight regarding human relations among target peoples in the immediate past is necessary.

4. For effective understanding of background conditions contributing to chronic social unrest in a target population, knowledge of recent developments may require considerable supplement from intimate knowledge of cultural organization and long-time social trends.

5. Any stimulus which confronts individuals in a target population with an acute sense of danger or its threat is a likely prelude to terror and panic, provided that responses to it have not been conventionalized, that it shatters immediately antecedent forms of behavior, and that it has sufficient duration, sequence, or repetition for the compounding of terror responses.

6. Any stimulus which, prior to its appearance, has been linguistically defined as acutely terrifying and unmanageable may induce immediate terror and guide action directly to flight.

7. The disruptive influences of shock appear to be greatest where surprise is most complete, where normal sensory functioning is inhibited, where the ratio of individuals suffering immediate personal or private property damage to the total population is greatest, where affected individuals respond most slowly or reluctantly to institutionalized commands, where physical protection is least adequate, and where affected individuals are in motion, particularly in retreat, at the moment of the crisis-provoking stimulus.

8. Following the initial shock produced by a crisis stimulus, a rapid sequence of inconsistent or contra-

dictory suggestions as to the meaning of the stimulus, or what to do about it, will compound confusion.

9. Terror is compounded by effective countermeasures to panic prevention or restriction devices.

10. Terror varies inversely with the number and adequacy of available escape outlets.

11. The incidence of shock, confusion, and terror in a population acutely aware of a crisis stimulus usually decreases as distance from the stimulus increases.

12. Effective models for terror and panic behavior stress immediately personal or egocentric rather than group or team goals, and, by suggesting flight, they tend to defeat efforts to maintain or re-establish order and to counteract appeals for cooperation.

13. Panic develops only when possible avenues for escape become evident.

14. Model suggestions for the extension and direction of panic movement are effective when rout is in process as well as when it begins.

15. Terror-augmenting stimuli that appear after general rout has begun reinforce flight suggestions and thus extend panic in time and space; for example, the probability of prolonged and extended terror and panic following an air raid would presumably be increased by secondary attacks on throngs of people rushing out along traffic arteries in quest of security.

16. The actions of people in panic are given common character by the identity or similarity in escape opportunities afforded by the setting in which rout proceeds and by exposure to common chains of social interaction.

17. Panic may be extended in time and space by the absence of diminution devices or by effective countermeasures to such devices.

18. Panic may be terminated by the relaxation of

threat, the attainment of safety, incapacitating injury, supervening fatigue, death, separation of individuals or small groups from an aggregate in rout, elimination of escape outlets, or effective substitution of some other action pattern.

19. Since acute fatigue, depression, anxiety, aggressive behavior, apprehensive rumors, social disruption, sickness, and injury are common, if transient, sequelae of terror and panic, these behavior forms might be most successfully provoked by directing acute danger threats to target populations recently terrorized or panicked.

The inference value of a series of propositions like the above, assuming that they are as concisely drawn as data permit, should increase almost geometrically as their number increases, and with this increase propositions might well fall into prime, corollary, and subordinate series. Scrutiny of the list of propositions here included should invite challenge, refinement, and extension by others who know other literature or by those who discern logical gaps and are thus led to further formulation. The present review has suggested several free theorizing leads of this latter sort, but these are not included here for the reason that the present obligation is to present, as concisely as possible, the inferences of concrete protocols. However, with this accomplished, the conclusion Robin Williams derived from his review of intergroup relations literature can very well be brought to bear on panic theory. Williams observed:

The sole aim of the compilation is to bring together in compact and convenient form a sampling of what is known and surmised in this field . . . Many, if not most, of the propositions outlined are at present little more than educated guesses . . . Nothing is to be gained in the current state of scientific knowledge in this field from the refusal to formulate hypotheses.[18]

The assumption, stated above, that the inference value of propositions about panic should increase almost geometrically as their number increases should hold even if the isolation of presumably relevant conditions and factors is but a first analytical step toward the end of purposive social control. Indeed, this isolation cannot specify how the concentration or combination of such elements affects the probability of the occurrence of terror or panic. This must await a much richer and tested body of principles. However, if knowledge about terror and panic must in a world of atomic bombs and guided missiles succeed sermonizing, the raw accretion of ideas and synthesis of such lore may emphasize what is not known as well as what is now known and assumed. Both may suggest next steps for development and testing of ideas.

[18] Robin M. Williams, Jr., *The Reduction of Intergroup Tensions* (New York: Social Science Research Council, 1947), pp. 49-50.

THE NATURE
AND CONDITIONS OF PANIC [1]
Enrico L. Quarantelli

Current conceptions of the nature and conditions of
panic are inadequate and lack an empirical basis. Using
data gathered by the Disaster Team of the National
Opinion Research Center and other documentary
sources, a comparative and analytical examination of
specific instances of the behavior is made. A conception
is developed of panic as the very antithesis of organized
group activity—as an acute fear reaction marked by
loss of self-control which is followed by nonsocial and
nonrational flight. Such behavior arises upon a definition of possible entrapment, a perception of collective
powerlessness, and a feeling of individual isolation in a
crisis.

On the basis of a comparative and analytical examination of specific instances of panic, the following discussion attempts to do two things: to present a systematic social psychological view of the nature of panic
and to outline the conditions associated with it.

Reprinted from the *American Journal of Sociology*, 1954, **60**, 267-275,
by permission of The University of Chicago Press and the author.
Copyright, 1954, The University of Chicago Press.

[1] Acknowledgment is made to the National Opinion Research Center
for permission to use the interview data on which this article is in
part based and from which all the quotations cited were taken. The
research by NORC was undertaken under a contract with the Army
Chemical Center, Department of the Army. However, the opinions
and conclusions expressed in this article are those of the author and
do not necessarily represent the views of NORC, the Army Chemical
Center, or the Department of the Army.

The author is also indebted to Rue Bucher and Charles Fritz for
valuable criticisms of a draft of the manuscript.

Current Conceptions about Panic

The fragmentary and scattered sociological and social psychological literature[2] on panic is almost completely nonempirical. With a few exceptions[3] it consists of: deductions from pre-existing theories of personality or social life which were developed quite independently of any firsthand study of panic; or unsystematic remarks based upon everyday preconceptions and unverified notions of what supposedly transpires when panics occur; or *ad hoc* statements representing impressionistic reflections on a few sparsely detailed accounts by observers of any one of the variety of activities that in popular parlance are termed panic. The lack of concrete, sufficient, and adequate empirical data (the gathering of which admittedly presents great practical and methodological difficulties) has prevented the setting up of a set of propositions about panic that have any implications for social theory, that are particularly useful for guiding research, or that have much value for social control.

Underscoring the inadequate understanding of the

[2] For reviews of the literature see E. L. Quarantelli, "A Study of Panic: Its Nature, Types, and Conditions" (unpublished Master's thesis, Department of Sociology, University of Chicago, 1953), pp. 1-39; Anselm L. Strauss, "The Literature on Panic," *Journal of Abnormal and Social Psychology*, XXXIX (1944), 317-28.

[3] See, for example, Paul B. Foreman, "Panic Theory," *Sociology and Social Research*, XXXVII (1953), 295-304; and Irving L. Janis, *Air War and Emotional Stress* (New York: McGraw-Hill, 1951), pp. 26-41, 43, 93-94, 161-62, 192-95. The discussions of both authors, especially the former, are considerably superior to most of the panic literature. Discussions based on experimental productions of so-called "panic" are presented by Alexander Mintz, "Non-Adaptive Group Behavior," *Journal of Abnormal and Social Psychology*, XLVI (1951), 150-59 and John French, Jr., "An Experimental Study of Group Panic," *Journal of the Elisha Mitchell Scientific Society*, LVII (1941), 195. For a better than average nonempirical discussion see Richard LaPiere, *Collective Behavior* (New York: McGraw-Hill, 1938), pp. 437-61.

phenomenon is the lack of agreement as to what the term "panic" means. The referent at times may be covert personal or collective moods and feelings; at other times overt individual or group actions and undertakings. Thus, basically dissimilar occurrences and events, such as a single individual's pathological anxiety and the institutionalized activities of a collectivity, are labeled and discussed as panic.[4]

As striking as the absence of a single referent is the lack of a set of distinctive criteria for distinguishing between panic as such and other related phenomena. To characterize panic, as is frequently done, as irrational, antisocial, impulsive, nonfunctional, maladaptive, inappropriate—apart from the hindsight evaluation and stereotypic imagery it implies—is of little assistance in classifying a particular individual or mass act. Such general terms are not criteria with which one can positively identify a concrete instance of behavior.

There is also wide disagreement on the conditions which produce or facilitate panic. Seldom is the same aspect even mentioned by more than a few students of the phenomenon. Consequently there is a great di-

---

[4] Almost every kind of socially disorganizing or personally disrupting type of activity has been characterized as panic. The range includes everything from psychiatric phenomena to economic phenomena (e.g., the "panics" involved in bank runs, stock-market crashes, depressions, etc.). Thus, in one recent book there are cited as instances of panic such phenomena as lynching mobs, suicidal epidemics, individual and collective anxieties, plundering troops, spy hysterias, military retreats and surrenders, social unrest, war, psychotic behavior, mass hysteria, animal stampedes, confused voting behavior, orgiastic feasts, the activities of war refugees, and group tensions. See Joost Meerloo, *Patterns of Panic* (New York: International Press, 1950). For one comparison of the typically diverse ways in which the term "panic" is used by different writers, see the various articles contained in *Transactions of the Conference on Morale and the Prevention and Control of Panic* (New York: New York Academy of Medicine and the Josiah Macy, Jr. Foundation, 1951).

vergency in emphasis concerning which factor or set of factors is responsible for panic.[5]

The inadequacy of knowledge about conditions underlying panic is particularly emphasized by two facts: the failure to maintain levels of analysis and the lack of specificity in the factors advanced. Physical, physiological, biopsychological, psychological, and sociological factors are all discussed as if they were one. They are treated as if they were at a same general and interchangeable level of analysis rather than being incommensurable and logically belonging to distinct and distinguishable planes of phenomena. Moreover, almost all of the diverse factors noted could just as well be stimulative conditions for phenomena that no one would seriously call panic.

The following analysis of panic, while based on empirical data, should be considered but a first step in an attempt to set panic behavior within existing theoretical conceptions and to provide observations and propositions for guidance and testing in future research.

Sources of Data

The data have been gathered from two sources. The main body of it is from the tape-recorded, nondirective type of interview gathered by the Disaster Team

---

[5] The causative conditions specified by various writers include such diverse factors as: the presence of crowd conditions, the state of the weather, deficiency in the organism of a specific vitamin, psychological isolation, mental contagion, fatigue, suggestion and heightened imitation, social unrest, hunger, the shattering of group solidarity or group bonds, the presence of predisposed personalities, lack or loss of leadership, emotional instability, poor group morale, lack of critical ability, fear, mimicry, emotional tension, crisis situations, lack of personal and collective discipline, uncertainty, anxiety, etc. For one listing and an insightful discussion of the inadequacy of the "causes" of panic as advanced by seventeen primarily military writers see Strauss, *op. cit.*

of the National Opinion Research Center. For the purposes of this study over 150 of these interviews, averaging about an hour and a half in length, were analyzed. Almost all of them were gathered in connection with disasters in which the writer participated in the field work and personally obtained a number of the interviews. Three events provided the bulk of the data. These were: a series of house explosions in Brighton, New York, September 21, 1951; a plane crash into a residential area in Elizabeth, New Jersey, February 11, 1952; and an earthquake in Bakersfield, California, August 22, 1952. The rest of the analyzed interview data was drawn from such disasters as tornadoes in Arkansas and Minnesota, a coal-mine explosion in West Frankfort, Illinois, a plane crash into a crowd in Flagler, Colorado, hotel and rooming house fires in Chicago, two other plane crashes into residential districts in Elizabeth, New Jersey, and a plant explosion in Minneapolis. This primary source of data was supplemented by carefully evaluated material found in documentary sources dealing with individual and group behavior in dangerous situations. A case-study analysis was made of over two hundred participant and eyewitness accounts of crises in many of which panic had occurred.

The Nature of Panic

Overt features.—The outstanding feature of panic, so far as outward observation is concerned, is flight. While such behavior is not peculiar to panic, it is nonetheless an ever present feature of the phenomenon whenever it occurs. It most frequently takes the form of actual physical running. However, it may also be manifested in varying activities such as driving vehicles, swimming, crawling, riding horses, rowing, climbing, jumping, digging, etc. This variety in the expressions of flight is possible because most socially learned and culturally ingrained motor patterns of action continue to be available to individuals in panic. Participants in such behavior do not revert or regress to acting in infantile or purely biologically patterned ways. However, since the majority of situations wherein panics occur do not lend themselves to non-running activities, panic flight is generally manifested in running.

The flight behavior is always oriented with reference to a threatening situation; that is, people in panic flee from a general locale, such as a collapsing building or a gas-filled house. Usually this involves movement away from specific perilous objects: panic participants thus run away from, for example, that section of a building which is on fire. However, if a perilous object lies between presumed safety and the endangered persons, the flight may be in the direction of a specific peril. Thus, people in panic may run toward danger objects if escape from the threatening situation lies in the same direction (e.g., toward sheets of flame if the only known exit from a building is on the other side). Much panic fleeing which from an outside observer's viewpoint appears to be blind fleeing into danger is probably of this nature. At any rate, panic flight is not random or helter-skelter; the participants do not run every which way but instead take their general orientation for flight from the threatening situation.

In the determination of the particular direction of flight (e.g., which exit an individual will attempt to escape through) two factors are often involved. These are (1) a habitual pattern and (2) the course of the interaction among individuals following the definition of the situation as dangerous. The former factor is exemplified by the cases of some housewives at Brighton who fled out of the frequently used but more distant back door, rather than the infrequently used but nearer front door of their homes. The latter factor is typified in the remarks of a worker after a plant explosion. Upon regaining consciousness he noted: "There was a gush of flame and smoke coming up the elevator shaft. I just started running. Lots of other people were running too. That's how I knew where to go." This interactional factor, however, is operative and influential only within the confines of the actual physical setting participants find themselves in at the time of crisis. Thus if there is only one apparent or known exit, it is in that direction that people will flee. Only when the physical setting presents possible alternative opportunities to escape can social interaction influence the particular direction of flight.

The general and directional orientation of panic flight to a threatening situation is related to the fact that in panic behavior there is no overt attempt to deal directly with the danger itself. Instead, the only overt action taken is escape or personal removal from the threat. No attempt is made to control the danger, to act toward it, or to manipulate it in any way. As one housewife who went to investigate a hissing she heard coming from a heating unit stated it: "As soon as I realized the gas was escaping from the hot-water heater I thought my house was going to blow up. I just picked up and ran out."

Frequently the flight of panic is the most adaptive course of action that could be undertaken in a particular situation. Thus, to flee from a building whose walls are tottering from an earthquake is on most occasions the most appropriate and effective behavior possible. In such instances the panic flight is functional, if functionality under such circumstances is thought of as activity which from an objective point of view is appropriate to survival. Similarly, not all panic behavior is collectively maladaptive. There are occasions where flight simultaneously engaged in by a number of people not only is appropriate in itself but also has no antisocial consequences. For example, the mass fleeing of the separated householders from their gas-filling houses at Brighton was no hindrance to the fleeing of any other person. There was no bodily contact of a destructive sort on the part of the individuals running out of their homes. The flight behavior there, as it is in many and probably most panics, was personally functional and in no way socially maladaptive to the situation. It is only in the very rare instance that panic takes the form of a crowd of individuals trampling over one another like animals in a wild stampede.

Panic, rather than being antisocial, is nonsocial behavior; ordinary social relationships are disregarded and pre-existent group action patterns fail to be applied.[6] This disintegration of social norms and cessation of action with reference to a group or institutional pattern sometimes results in the shattering of the strongest primary group ties and the ignoring of the most expected behavior patterns. Thus, there is the case of the woman who, thinking a bomb had hit her house, fled in panic, leaving her baby behind, and returned only when she redefined the situation as an explosion across the street. As she stated it, the explosion

---

[6] This does not mean that social interaction does not sometimes occur among participants at the height of panic flight. However, such interaction as does take place is at a very elementary level. It does not involve responding to other individuals in their usual social roles.

shook the house. The first thing I thought of was a bomb. I just felt it was a bomb and I ran out. I was in my bathrobe. You don't think of anything save to get out—just to get out. I ran out and the house over there was flames from the bottom to the top so I ran back and grabbed the baby out of his crib.

This nonsocial aspect may be short-lived but it is this feature which, even at an overt level, distinguishes many cases of panic from controlled withdrawal behavior. In the case of controlled withdrawal, confused, random, ill-co-ordinated activity may be manifested, but the normal social bonds and the conventional interactional patterns are not totally disregarded. Thus, when a plane hit an apartment house in Elizabeth, most families evacuated as units, neighbors were warned, alternative courses of action were discussed, etc. People were running around and there was much confusion and partially unorganized activity but the whole structure of social relations normally guiding human behavior did not collapse as it does when full panic flight occurs.

Thus, panic flight represents very highly individualistic behavior. It involves completely individual as over against group action in coping with the problem of escape from a danger. In the case of panic there is no unity of action, no co-operation with others, no joint activity by the members of the mass; there is a total breakdown of corporate or concerted behavior. In short, panic flight is the very antithesis of organized group behavior.

Covert features.—Panic participants invariably define the situation as highly and personally dangerous. Whether this be arrived at individually or collectively, panic participants always perceive a direct threat to physical survival. This experiencing of extreme danger

to bodily safety is exemplified in the following remarks
by a man who looked up and saw a flaming plane div-
ing toward the street where he was pushing a wheel-
barrow:

> This thing seemed to me as if it was coming right at
> me. I ran like a scared rabbit across the street. My push-
> cart—I abandoned that to save my neck. I was scared.
> This thing went up in a big puff of flame and gasoline.
> It exploded. All I was thinking was that this big ball of
> gasoline was coming down on top of me and I was mak-
> ing a run in order to get away from it. I was running
> pell-mell across the street. I was looking at this big ball
> as I was running like a scared rabbit for fear it was
> going to pounce on my head, you know. The only thing
> I was thinking as I was running across and I was look-
> ing up at this big ball of fire, I was thinking to myself,
> I wonder if any part of this is going to hit me?

Furthermore, as the above quotation indicates, the
orientation of attention of panic participants is always
to the future, to what subsequently may be endangering. Attention is never directed to what had already
happened. Rather it is focused on what may happen.
Thus, during an earthquake a panic participant perceives that (to paraphrase many) "if I stay here I will
be killed." It is always anticipatory rather than retrospective perceptions of danger that accompany panic
activity.

Panic participants see the potential threat as very
immediate and survival dependent on a very rapid
reaction. A laborer caught in a plant explosion who
fled in panic said, after he recovered consciousness:
"When I came to, the dust and minerals and everything was crashing all around. My first thought was
that something would fall on me and finish me. My
main thought was to figure a way to get out."

Not only do panic participants know what they are immediately afraid *for* (which is their own physical safety), but they also are aware of what they are afraid *of*. The fear[7] that is experienced in panic is of something specific, of something which can be designated. The covert reaction of the individual in panic is never in regard to the unknown or the incomprehensible as such. It is always of a specific threat, the particularization of which may be arrived at individually or through social interaction.

Related to this is that in defining the situation panic participants see the threat as associated with a definite place. In fact, individuals will continue to flee in panic only to the extent they believe themselves within a danger area and still exposed to the consequences of the threat. As one worker who fled after a factory explosion expressed it: "My idea was to get away from the building because I had in mind it might fall. At the time I knew I was in danger of death but after I got out of the building I felt I was out of danger." This individual only stopped running after he had removed himself from inside the building which he had defined as the place of danger. (However, in panic the threat is not necessarily associated with being inside

---

[7] Fear, rather than anxiety, is the affective component of the panic reaction. Along one dimension, at least, fear and anxiety may be thought of as poles of a continuum. This is in regard to the specificity of a threat from the viewpoint of the individual. The fear-stricken individual perceives some highly ego-involved value greatly endangered. The threat is something that can be labeled, localized in space, and therefore potentially can be escaped from. The threat is specific. In contrast, there is no such recognition and judgment by the anxiety-stricken person. Anxiety is marked by an inability to designate any object in the environment to account for the diffuse sense of foreboding or even dread the individual is experiencing. This inability prevents any attempts at flight, for physical withdrawal requires a specific object or situation from which an orientation can be taken. See Kurt Riezler, "The Social Psychology of Fear," *American Journal of Sociology*, XLIX (1944), 489-98; and Rollo May, *The Meaning of Anxiety* (New York: Ronald, 1950), pp. 46-58.

a structure. Any open area during a machine-gun strafing, for example, may be viewed as a place of danger.)
But whether it be inside or outside, panic participants
always see the threat as present at or quickly reaching
the place where they are or will be.

Now people do not usually flee in panic from a
threatening situation. Individuals may feel extreme
fear and yet engage in a variety of nonpanic behavior
including, for example, direct action against the danger. To the extent they do so it is because they check
their fear, i.e., their impulse to run from the threatening situation.[8] Self-control is maintained.

Conversely, in panic there is a collapse of existing
curbs on the impulse to flee. The participant is the
individual who has lost self-control over his fear. For
example, one woman expressed her feeling of fear just
before she fled in panic as follows:

> You wanted to just get away. I felt I wanted to go. I
> wanted to run. Get away. Get away. I thought if that
> house goes the one next to me is going to go too and
> I'd be in the center of it. I heard the crash, the house
> went up [i.e., exploded] and I went.

A concomitant of the loss of self-control is that the
orientation of activity of the panic participant becomes highly self-centered. The fleeing individual
thinks only of saving himself. This egocentric attitude
is a counterpart of the individualism of the overt
flight behavior previously noted. Subjectively it involves a complete focusing upon the idea of getting
one's self out of the threatening situation: "All I
thought about was getting out of there," said a girl

---

[8] Young notes that "for human subjects to designate an experience as
fear, the presence of an escape impulse is required." See Paul T.
Young, *Emotion in Man and Animal* (New York: John Wiley & Sons,
1943), p. 197.

who fled in panic from a building during an earth-quake.

The focusing of thought, however, does not mean that the participant acts only reflexively or instinctively and is totally unaware of anything else. If the individual is going to engage in flight at all there has to be sufficient awareness to perceive *and* to continue to define a situation as a highly threatening one. A certain minimal awareness is also indicated by the fact that he does not run blindly into a wall; he heads for a door; and he goes around objects and obstacles in his path rather than attempting to crash through them. Moreover, when fleeing in a collective panic, the participant is at least partially aware of the presence of others although he may not directly respond to their activities.

However, to state that panic flight involves a degree of awareness on the part of participants is not to suggest in any way that it is a highly rational activity. It certainly does *not* involve the weighing of alternative lines of action. As a woman who fled in panic during an earthquake said: "The first thought you have is to run. I had that thought. I ran." On the other hand, panic flight does not involve irrational thought if by that is meant anything in the way of faulty deductions from certain premises. From the position of an outside observer this may appear to be the case but, from a participant's viewpoint, given his limited perspective of only certain portions of the total situation, no such interpretation of irrationality can be made. For the fleeing person, his action appears to him quite appropriate to the situation as he perceives it at that time.

Actually, rather than being rational or irrational, panic behavior is nonrational. Panic participants focus on the idea of fleeing but they do not take into account the consequences of their action (which may be even more dangerous than the panic-inciting threat itself). Faced with the immediate possibility of personal annihilation they do not consider possible alternative lines of action to flight.

To summarize: panic can be defined as an acute fear reaction marked by a loss of self-control which is followed by nonsocial and nonrational flight behavior. Covertly there is an acute fear reaction, i.e., an intense impulse to run from an impending danger. Panic participants are seized by fear of a specific object defined as involving an immediate and extreme physical threat. The most striking overt feature is flight behavior which, while not necessarily nonfunctional or maladaptive, always involves an attempt to remove one's self physically. Thus panic is marked by loss of self-control, that is, by unchecked fear, being expressed in flight. Two other prominent features are nonrational thought and nonsocial behavior: panic participants do not weigh the social consequences of their flight and are highly individualistic and self-centered in their actions with reference to one another. There is no consideration of alternative courses of action to flight. Thought being focused on the removal of one's self from danger, the ordinary social norms and interactional patterns are ignored and there is no possibility of group action.

Conditions for Panic

Panics occur following crises[9] in which the danger

---

[9] Broadly conceived, a crisis is produced by an interruption of an habitual or on-going line of action. The interruption need not be of a violent nature. Any crisis, however, is marked by a focusing of attention on the introjected stimulation and attempts at adjustive behavior. From its very nature it necessitates some reorientation of activity on the part of involved individuals. See W. I. Thomas, *Source Book for Social Origins* (Boston: Gorham, 1909), pp. 17-18.

is defined as an immediate and potential threat to the bodily self. However, panic flight is only one possible outcome in such situations. In the face of a threat, the potential courses of action available range from direct attack to movement away from the danger object.[10] If self-control is maintained there may be controlled withdrawal. That is, fear impulses may be curbed to the extent that the usual social bonds and relationships are maintained while physical separation from the danger is effected in conjunction with others. What then are the specific conditions under which movement away from threat during a crisis will change into panic flight? When does self-control break down in a dangerous crisis?

Specific conditions for the development of panic.—

---

[10] It may be noted that, generally speaking, except among the military where the group response has been highly conventionalized, there exist no institutional patterns for meeting such situations. In the somewhat special area of military panic, a number of case-study analyses were made in the course of our study. However, relatively little material suitable for analytical treatment could be found. The bulk of the not inconsiderable theoretical literature on military panic (especially in French and German sources) is highly speculative and abstract in nature and generally of a summarizing rather than analytical nature. For one such recent summary statement on panic by military men see John Caldwell, Stephen Ransom, and Jerome Sacks, "Group Panic and Other Mass Disruptive Reactions," *U.S. Armed Forces Medical Journal*, II (1951), 541-67. Actual descriptions of military panics either by participants or eyewitnesses are difficult to find. See, however, the excellent firsthand accounts given in Jack Belden, *Still Time To Die* (New York: Harper, 1944), esp. pp. 141-46, 163-67. Most of the secondhand or generalized accounts that are available are of limited research usefulness because of the inaccuracy and/or inadequacy of the materials. See, however, C. T. Lanham, "Panic," *Infantry Journal*, XLIV (1937), 301-8.

In so far as any statement can be made on the basis of the scanty reliable data, it would seem that military panics are the same in nature and development as panic in general. Consideration of the data suggests, however, the necessity of one precondition for the emergence of military panic. Normally, military groups function collectively and effectively as a matter of routine in the face of very extreme personal dangers. Only where there is an absence or breakdown of this normal military group solidarity is panic possible. For a further discussion of this point see Quarantelli, *op. cit.*, pp. 110-20.

The most important condition for the occurrence and continuance of panic is the feeling on the part of a participant that he may be unable to escape from an impending threat. Whether it be individually or collectively reached, this feeling of possible entrapment predominates from the first and prevails throughout panic flight. As one person stated it: "I didn't even think anything except getting myself out. From the time I left my bed to the door that's the only thing I could think of—am I going to get out? Am I going to be trapped?"

The important aspect is the belief or feeling of *possible* entrapment. This is reiterated again and again in the remarks of panic participants. It is not that affected individuals believe or feel they are definitely trapped. In such instances panic does not follow, as in the case of the woman who said: "I felt like I was trapped. I really knew there was trouble but I didn't know where to run." The flight of panic arises only when being trapped is sensed or thought of as a possibility rather than an actuality.[11]

The feeling of possibly being trapped does not necessarily (although this is most frequently the case) involve actual physical obstacles to movement. War refugees caught in the open by strafing planes can develop as acute a sense of potential entrapment as individuals inside a building during an earthquake who see all exits becoming blocked by falling debris.

Furthermore, it is only when actual or presumed

---

[11] This conclusion was arrived at by the author prior to his knowledge that Foreman had also reached a very similar but differently approached conclusion. In his words, "panic develops only when possible avenues for escape become evident" (op. cit., p. 303). This idea that panic arises only when entrapment and escape are perceived as possible runs quite counter to one of the most dominant notions about the genesis of panic behavior, i.e., that it arises when a person is completely trapped in a dangerous situation.

blockage of escape to safety is related to immediate consequences that the feeling of entrapment plays a part in the generation of panic flight. Coal miners entombed by a collapsed tunnel who recognize they will have sufficient air till rescuers can dig through to them do not panic. Only when being trapped is seen as something that is going to involve immediate personal danger will it possibly initiate flight behavior. Such occurred in the following instance related by an individual who was on the top story of a factory shattered by an explosion: "Six or eight of us became panicky when we found the stairways blocked by chunks of concrete. The dust, which looked like smoke, made us think that the building was in flames below us." In this particular instance the behavior evolved into only rudimentary collective panic. The important point, however, is that the behavior started to take that form because the men thought themselves possibly trapped atop a burning building. As in all instances of panic, they reacted to the immediate dangerous consequences of possible entrapment (i.e., being burned, etc.) rather than to being trapped as such.

Most frequently the feeling of possible entrapment arises in the course of interaction with other persons in the same situation. Yet it may be individually arrived at, especially in the face of a very sudden and highly dangerous crisis such as a sharp earthquake. However, the more progressive the crisis, the greater the possibility that interaction with others will lead to a definition of the situation as one involving potential entrapment.

The other specific condition which is necessary although not unique to the occurrence and development of panic is a feeling of great helplessness. This condition has two components: a feeling of impotency or powerlessness and a sense of "aloneness."

Faced with a necessity of acting, the individual feels he may be unable to prevent the consequences of the impending danger from occurring. This feeling of powerlessness has nothing to do with the capability of a fear-stricken person to flee. Thus, a woman reported:

> When I realized the gas was escaping from the hot-water heater I knew it wasn't anything to monkey with, something not to play with. I *knew* that an accumulation of gas would blow up. I mean water you could cope with, dumping it out or something, but with gas I don't know anything. I thought my house was going to blow up. I was really scared. I ran out.

Persons in panic feel powerless to bring the threat itself under control but they do not despair of getting out of danger by fleeing.

Very often the feeling of personal powerlessness is greatly reinforced by social interaction. At first individuals may feel individually powerless and be greatly afraid. Yet they may expect or hope others will be able to cope with the danger. When the responses of the others, however, indicate that they, too, are powerless or have even suffered the consequences, panic becomes probable. As an individual caught in explosions in a factory stated it: "I can truthfully say when I heard the moaning and crying of the others I did get quite panicky. I was rather anxious to see which way I could get out." More frequently there is verbal communication about the potential danger.

The other important aspect of the sense of helplessness is the feeling of isolation or "aloneness." It is the realization that one has to act and to depend upon one's self alone to find a way to safety. As a woman who was working in a plant with a number of other women when an earthquake struck said:

> When it started shaking so bad I noticed that I was there by myself. I felt even more scared. When you're by yourself in something like that and there's nobody to depend on. There was nobody around. I don't know where they disappeared to. I didn't see nobody. I ran out.

In all cases of panic, this feeling of "aloneness" or sole dependency on one's own action is present to some degree.

Contributory panic conditions.—One of the most important contributory conditions is the existence of a social or group predefinition of a crisis as one that is likely to eventuate in panic flight. Of some crises, people have certain preconceptions of their dangerousness because of the probable behavior of others in the circumstances.[12] The simplest example is the belief that a fire in a crowded place is especially dangerous because, among other things, panic is probable. Any such predefining of a situation as potentially panic-producing can have a direct effect on a participant's interpretation of the behavior of others, as well as on his own behavior. He may start to withdraw in order not to get caught in the expected panic. If many of those present do the same, the withdrawing of each person reinforces the like belief of everyone else that what thy feared is actually happening. Thus, ordinary withdrawal can become panic flight.

---

[12] Alfred Lindesmith and Anselm Strauss note that individuals "become panicked in situations which have previously been linguistically defined as fearful or terrifying." See their *Social Psychology* (New York: Dryden, 1949), p. 332.

Another contributory condition to panic is a previous crisis that leaves those who have experienced it highly sensitized to signs indicative of a recurrence. This often leads them to prepare to flee immediately upon noting any cues indicative of a possible recurrence of the threat. As one resident of Brighton stated a few days after the widespread gas explosions:

> Every time we smell a little smoke or we think we smell a little gas or hear noises, such as probably every-day noises that we never noticed before—because everybody is on the alert now—we're all ready to get out of the house.

However, perceptual hypersensitivity is not in itself generally determinative of panic behavior. Whether flight will occur or not depends upon the interaction following the initiation of the crisis; "panic-ripeness" is not enough.

To summarize: panic develops as a result of a feeling of possible entrapment, a perception of collective powerlessness, and a feeling of individual isolation in a crisis situation. Important in the generation, emergence, and persistence of these factors is social interaction. Without such interaction, panic is not impossible, especially if there is a very sudden crisis situation, but it is much less likely to occur. The chances for the development of the above conditions, which form the basis for the loss of self-control, are considerably enhanced when agitated individuals in a dangerous situation are interacting with one another.

However, this does not mean that panic in a particular crisis excludes the concurrent existence of other forms of behavior. An individual may be in panic when the man next to him is not: any widespread dangerous situation will usually evoke a full range of noninstitutionalized to routinized or habitual behavior.

The frequency of panic has been over-exaggerated. In the literature on disasters, for example, so much emphasis is placed on it that one easily gets the impression that it is the most common and important immediate reaction to such crisis situations. This is not the case. Compared with other reactions panic is a relatively uncommon phenomenon.

OVERVIEW

Duane P. Schultz

All of the theories dealing with panic in unorganized groups invoke one or more of the following five variables: (1) perception of a crisis situation, (2) intense fear, (3) antecedent or background factors, (4) mutual emotional facilitation or behavioral contagion, and (5) breakdown in mutual cooperation.

Of these variables only two (perception of a crisis situation, and fear) are discussed by every theorist. But as mentioned in Chapter I, evidence indicates that the existence of a crisis and its accompanying emotion of fear will not always lead to nonadaptive flight behavior. The work of Janis (1951) in his analysis of the Hiroshima bombing is again cited in support of this contention. That perception and definition of crisis, as well as fear, are necessary conditions for panic to develop cannot be denied, but analysis of the theories of panic suggests that other variables must also be operative.

Although some form of behavioral contagion is invoked by McDougall, LaPiere, Foreman, and Quarantelli as regards the genesis and spread of panic behavior, Cantril does not discuss this factor while

Mintz feels it to be inessential. And indeed even those theorists who do discuss it agree that its impact is felt only *after* the perception and definition of the crisis situation, when it then functions to compound and spread the fear and terror among all those present in the crowd. Its suggested role, then, is at least that of facilitating, if not actually precipitating, panic flight. The mutual emotional facilitation serves as a terror-reinforcing agent—reinforcing and perhaps giving concrete expression to each individual's own fear. But what it is that causes those few individuals in the very early phase of a crisis to express their fear overtly, and in so doing to spread the behavior through the entire group, still remains a moot point.

To three of our theorists, the answer lies in certain background or antecedent factors of the individual group members themselves. Certain individuals are more suggestible (Cantril) or are weakened physically and/or emotionally (Foreman) so that they are less capable of rationally interpreting the situation. Also, Quarantelli notes that a preconception or predefinition of a situation as potentially panic-producing can influence a person's interpretation of the behavior of others. Thus, as suggested by Brown (1954), and as will be discussed in Chapter V, there may exist certain individuals who are "panic-prone," in which case research on the individual threshold for mob behavior may be in order, to identify the characteristics of the "panic-prone" individual.

A final variable—breakdown in mutual consideration—is mentioned by all but Cantril. Mintz suggests that panic will arise *only* when a few members of a crowd cease to cooperate.

At this stage of our understanding, it would be gratuitous to suggest that any one of these variables is more important than another. It would seem that panic will proceed more readily when all of these variables are operating concurrently. In this regard it is to be noted that only Foreman and Quarantelli invoke all of these variables as causal or contributory conditions of panic behavior.

III

Panic in Organized Groups

SIGMUND FREUD'S THEORY

The focus for the majority of panic theorists has been only on unorganized crowds. To date, only two theoretical efforts have been specifically addressed to panic in organized groups: that of Sigmund Freud in 1922, and Duane P. Schultz in 1964, both of which efforts are concerned with panic in the military.

In Freud's book, *Group Psychology and the Analysis of the Ego,* he suggests that panic behavior can be best studied in military groups. He considers an army, like a church, to be a highly artificial grouping in that some external force is required to keep it intact and to maintain its rigid structural integrity. As the group owes its continuing existence to the illusory existence of a leader who loves all the group members with an equal love, libidinal ties thus develop between the members and the leader, as well as among the members themselves.

Panic arises, according to Freud, when this group

disintegrates to the point where: (1) the orders of the superior are no longer attended to, and (2) each individual becomes concerned with his own welfare only and has no consideration for the other members.

But what causes the group to disintegrate? It is not the perception of a crisis or of danger, *per se*, says Freud, because military units may hitherto have faced equal or even greater danger and still remained intact and performed successfully. Panic results, rather, from a relaxation or breakdown of the libidinal structure of the group. Freud comments in this respect that "Dread in an individual is provoked either by the greatness of a danger or by the cessation of emotional ties. . . . In just the same way panic arises either owing to an increase of the common danger or owing to the disappearance of the emotional ties which hold the group together" (1922, p. 48). However, the specific cause(s) of the breakdown of the libidinal (emotional) structure, Freud does not make clear.

In Schultz's article, "Panic in Organized Collectivities," panic is again considered to result from a breakdown in group structure; however, the psychoanalytic concept of libidinal ties is not invoked. Rather, the group is discussed in perhaps more operational terms of group cohesion.

According to Schultz, panic flight follows from a breakdown in group cohesiveness. As to what causes this breakdown, he discusses a number of predispositional and precipitating variables as causal factors. The idea of a breakdown in mutual consideration as a necessary precursor of panic is not unique with Schultz. Quarantelli (1954), for example, in a brief reference to military panics, has similarly noted that panic is possible only when there is a breakdown of normal military group solidarity.

The concept of group cohesiveness is readily amenable to experimentation in that it is capable of quan-
tification and experimental manipulation.

PANIC IN ORGANIZED
COLLECTIVITIES
Duane P. Schultz

One aspect of group behavior which has received little
attention is that of panic behavior. The existing literature has tended to focus on panic in unorganized mobs
or crowds. The analyses of the panic behavior in the
famous Coconut Grove Fire (Veltford & Lee, 1943)
and the "Invasion from Mars" broadcast (Cantril,
Gaudet & Herzog, 1940) are representative of this type
of study.

It is the purpose of this paper to review the literature on panic in organized collectivities, i.e., military
groups, and to present a theoretical framework within
which this behavioral phenomenon may be explained.

Examination of the literature on military panic re-
veals little substantive material suitable to analytic
treatment. For the most part, the literature is very
speculative and abstract in nature. With a few exceptions (Belden, 1944; Marshall, 1947) it is difficult to
find actual descriptions of military panics either by
participants or by eyewitnesses. Most of the generalized accounts to be found are of limited utility be-

Reprinted in part from the *Journal of Social Psychology*, 1964, **63**,
53-359, by permission of The Journal Press and the author. Copyright, 1964, by The Journal Press.

cause of their inaccuracy and/or inadequacy (Quarantelli, 1954).

The Nature of Panic

In his excellent analysis of the nature of panic
Quarantelli (1954) examined both overt and cover
features of panic. The most outstanding overt feature
was found to be flight from a threatening situation
Hence, in panic, there is no attempt to control or
manipulate the threat where there is this possibility
"The only action taken toward the threat is to get
away from it" (Quarantelli, 1954).

Quarantelli (1954) conceives of panic as being non
social rather than antisocial, i.e., there is a complete
breakdown in group cohesion and there is no attempt
to act jointly or in cooperation with others.

As to the covert features of panic, Quarantelli
(1954) noted that the prime factor is a very direct
and immediate sense of threat to physical survival
leading to intense fear and loss of self-control. Quarantelli also suggests that panic is non-rational rather
than irrational in that panic participants do not consider the consequences of their flight behavior nor do
they consider alternative courses of action.

Conditions Causing Panic

There exists a wide spectrum of opinion in the literature as to the causes of military panic. The one theme
prevalent in most discussions of military panic is that
of fear and the immediate threat to physical survival
Loss of confidence in the group's leader is often mentioned as a cause (Andrews, 1920; Brousseau, 1920
Coste, 1929; Cygielstrejch, 1916; Maxwell, 1923; Rick
man, 1938; Schmideberg, 1939; and Strauss, 1944,
LaPiere (1938), Farago (1942), Stone (1941) an

Caldwell, Ranson & Sachs (1951) consider the perception of a threat for which there is no prepared or routinized behavior as a prime cause. Prolonged waiting in anticipation of battle is noted as a cause by Eltlinge (1917), Brousseau (1920) and Farago (1942).

Some writers have stressed individual predispositions to panic. Strauss (1944), in surveying this literature, divided these factors into the following: (1) those that physically weaken men; like intoxication, bad health, poor nourishment, or fatigue, (2) those that lessen mental ability; like confusion, doubt, and uncertainty, (3) those that produce high emotional tension and heightened imagination.

Foreman (1953) lists the following predisposing conditions to panic: (1) acute fatigue which weakens individuals organically, (2) worry about lack of information concerning expected attacks which creates acute emotional tensions and anxiety, (3) novice or stranger status which prevents or impoverishes self-satisfying group identifications, (4) awareness of such weapons as guided missiles and napalm which incite chronic social unrest.

Discussion

Thus, the literature suggests the operation of a set of variables which may predispose an organized collectivity to panic flight. Foreman (1953) noted that Although background conditions are not causal factors of panic, deliberate attempts to induce or reinforce terror or panic should succeed more readily where conditions known to be present in prior instances are clearly present and compounded." These predispositional variables would seem to operate to weaken men both physically and psychologically and to cause them to be more easily influenced by rumor and suggestion and render them less capable of rationally interpreting ambiguous situations.

The literature also suggests the operation of certain variables which are capable of precipitating panic flight, either in combination with the predispositional variables or independently if of sufficient intensity.

Brown (1954) noted that practically every writer on panic invokes at least one principle of contagion. Imitation, mimicry, and suggestion are mentioned by Percin (1914), Eltlinge (1917), Brousseau (1920), Munson (1921), Maxwell (1923), Coste (1929), Strauss (1944), Caldwell, Ranson & Sachs (1951), and Quarantelli (1954). In an investigation of seven panic incidents in World II, Marshall (1947) found that each incident had the same origin; the sight of a few members of the group in full and unexplained flight to the rear. One or a few men made a sudden run to the rear which others in the vicinity did not understand. "In every case, the testimony of all the witnesses clearly developed the fact that those who started to run, and thereby spread the fear which started the panic, had a legitimate, or at least a reasonable excuse, for the action. It was not the sudden motion which of itself did the damage but the fact that others present were not kept informed" (Marshall 1947, p. 146). Unfortunately, these accounts gave no indication of the existence of any of the predispositional variables discussed above.

The second precipitating variable involves the exposure to a threat (i.e., weapon) for which there is no prepared behavior. This was exemplified in the First World War when the Germans introduced two new and (at the time) terrifying weapons for which there had been no training on the part of the Allied troops—gas warfare and the flammenwerfer (flame thrower). A complete panic flight was the result with those who survived the initial assaults by these weapons (Auld, 1918). In subsequent exposures, however, after informational and training programs had been given the Allied troops, the incidence of panic was extremely rare. The troops had learned of the nature of the weapons and how to cope with them.

With respect to the predispositional variables, the point is made that all the factors mentioned above are found by definition in combat at one time or another. Yet, history does not record a high incidence of panic among military groups. That these conditions have been noted in troops who have panicked seems to be true but that military units have experienced these conditions, often to a high degree of intensity, and not panicked is equally true. To what, then, can be attributed the occurrence of panic behavior in military groups?

An explanatory model based upon the concept of group cohesiveness is offered. Cartwright and Zander (1953) discuss a cohesive group as one in which the members all work together for a common goal and everyone is ready to assume responsibility for the group tasks. "The willingness to endure pain or frustration for the group is yet another indication of cohesiveness. Finally, we may conceive of a cohesive group as one in which its members will defend against external criticism or attack" (Cartwright & Zander, 1953, p. 74). Adding the notions that: (1) the group may become a haven for protection from a threatening environment and thus become a means to satisfy the need for security (Grinker & Spiegel, 1945), and (2) there are external restraints which serve to keep the group intact; a small army unit would seem to reasonably fit the definition of a cohesive group.

It is but a short step to make the further assumption that the small cohesive army unit can be considered a primary group (Cooley, 1909) in that it is characterized by an intimate, face-to-face relationship, a warm emotional tone, and involves close physical proximity.

In a military environment, the individual soon finds himself isolated from his civilian primary group. Shils & Janowitz (1948) suggested that, as a result, the individual soldier comes to depend more and more upon his military primary group for satisfaction of basic needs, affection, security, status, etc. Serving to reinforce the satisfactions and the demands and expectations of this group are the officially prescribed rules and external authority which serve to hold his aggressiveness in its proper context.

Thus, in their analysis of the ability of the Wehrmacht to maintain a high degree of organizational integrity in spite of their continual strategic reverses, Shils & Janowitz (1948) conclude:

> Where conditions were such as to allow primary group life to function smoothly and where the primary group developed a high degree of cohesion, morale was high and resistance effective. . . . The motivation of the determined resistance of the German soldier was the steady satisfaction of certain primary personality demands afforded by the social organization of the army.

Accordingly, it is hypothesized that the "social disorganization of panic in organized collectivities is dependent to a large measure on the capacity of the immediate primary group to avoid social disintegration. When this primary group is able to adequately satisfy the individual's physiological and social-psychological needs, then the element of self-concern is minimized. Conversely, when the primary group life is disrupted by the predispositional and/or precipitating variables discussed above, an intensity of preoccupation with physical survival develops and the attraction to remain a member of the group is minimized.

Studies of combat personnel (Grinker & Spiegel, 1945) have emphasized the importance of group identification as a major motivational factor underlying efficient performance in the face of danger. Inherent in this is the notion that the tendency to abandon one's duty or to escape from the situation is often held in check by the strong motivation to avoid letting the other members of the group down.

An interesting heuristic outgrowth of this conceptualization would be a replication of the study by Mintz (1951) who suggested that the nonadaptive character of panic behavior can be explained in terms of the perceived reward structure of the situation. His results were interpreted as confirming the theory that panic results from the perception of an unstable reward structure. It would seem worthwhile to replicate Mintz's study using as *Ss* groups varying in degrees of cohesiveness. Such a study is now in progress.

Discussion of other theories which have been advanced to explain panic behavior is beyond the scope of the present paper. The reader is referred to McDougall (1920), Freud (1922), LaPiere (1938), Mintz (1951), and Foreman (1953).

References

ANDREWS, L. *Military manpower.* New York: Dutton, 1920.
AULD, S. J. M. *Gas and flame in modern warfare.* New York: George H. Doran Co., 1918.
BELDEN, J. *Still time to die.* New York: Harper & Bros., 1944.

BROUSSEAU, A. *Essai sur la peur aux armées, 1914-1918.* Paris: Alcan, 1920.

BROWN, R. W. Mass phenomena. In Lindzey, G., ed.: *Handbook of Social Psychology.* Reading, Mass.: Addison-Wesley, 1954, Ch. 23.

CALDWELL, J. M., RANSON, S. W. & SACHS, J. G. Group panic and other mass disruptive reactions. *U.S. Armed Forces med. J.,* 1951, 2, 541-567.

CANTRIL, H. The causes and control of riot and panic. *Public Opinion Quart.,* 1943, 7, 669-679.

CANTRIL, H., GAUDET, H. & HERZOG, H. *The invasion from Mars.* Princeton: Princeton Univ. Press, 1940.

CARTWRIGHT, D. & ZANDER, A. *Group dynamics: research and theory.* White Plains: Row, Peterson & Co., 1953.

COOLEY, C. H. *Social organization.* New York: Scribner, 1909.

COSTE, C. *Le psychologie du combat.* Paris: Berger-Levrault, 1929.

CYGIELSTREJCH, A. La psychologie de la panique pendant la guerre. *Année méd. Psychol.,* 1916, I, 176-192.

ELTLINGE, L. *The psychology of war.* Fort Leavenworth: Press of the Army Service School, 1917.

FARAGO, L., ed. *German psychological warfare,* 3rd ed. New York: Putnam, 1942.

FOREMAN, P. B. Panic theory. *Sociol. soc. Res.,* 1953, 37, 295-304.

FREUD, S. *Group psychology and the analysis of the ego.* London: Hogarth Press, 1922.

GRINKER, R. R. & SPIEGEL, J. P. *Men under stress.* Philadelphia: Blakeston Press, 1945.

JANIS, I. L. *Air war and emotional stress.* New York: McGraw-Hill, 1951.

LAPIERE, R. T. *Collective behavior.* New York: McGraw-Hill, 1938.

MARSHALL, S. L. A. *Men against fire.* New York: Morrow, 1947.

MAXWELL, W. N. *A psychological retrospect of the great war.* New York: Macmillan, 1923.

McDOUGALL, W. *The group mind.* Cambridge, Eng.: Cambridge Univ. Press, 1920.

MINTZ, A. Non-adaptive group behavior. *J. abnorm. soc. Psychol.,* 1951, 46, 150-159.

MUNSON, E. *The management of men.* New York: Holt, 1921.

PERCIN, A. *Le combat.* Paris: Alcan, 1914.

QUARANTELLI, E. The nature and conditions of panic. *Amer. J. Sociol.,* 1954, 60, 267-275.

RICKMAN, J. Panic and air raid precautions. *Lancet,* 1938, 1, 1291-1295.

SCHMIDEBERG, W. The treatment of panic in casualty area and clearing station. *Life & Letters Today*, 1939, 23, 162-169.

SHILS, E. & JANOWITZ, M. Cohesion and disintegration in the Wehrmacht in World War II. *Public Opinion Quart.*, 1948, 12, 280-315.

STONE, T. E. Man, fear, and panic. *Infantry Journal*, 1941, 349.

STRAUSS, A. L. The literature on panic. *J. abnorm. soc. Psychol.*, 1944, 39, 317-328.

VELTFORD, H. R. & LEE, S. E. The Coconut Grove Fire: A study in scapegoating. *J. abnorm. soc. Psychol.*, 1943, 38, 138-154.

IV

Behavior of
Panic Participants

DISCUSSION

BEHAVIOR OF PEOPLE IN
PANIC FLIGHT

In the following article, Enrico Quarantelli discusses the nature of the behavior of people engaged in panic flight, basing his observations on tape-recorded interviews of approximately 1,000 people who were involved in major and minor disasters studied by the Disaster Team of the National Opinion Research Center of the University of Chicago. Quarantelli's conception of panic in this article is broader than our definition discussed in Chapter I. Whereas our earlier definition restricts panic behavior to flight which is nonadaptive—that is, detrimental to the survival of the group—he considers both adaptive and nonadaptive flight behavior as characteristic of panic.

Quarantelli takes issue with the generally accepted image of a panic participant as one "who has been stripped down to sheer emotional reaction, or who has reverted to an animal-like level of response" (p. 188). Instead, he offers a series of propositions which characterize the panic participant as one who uses socially learned patterns of responses in order to arrive at his own individualistic resolution of the crisis. He suggests that the panicky person's behavior is not necessarily maladaptive from the standpoint of the group and that behavior in which people knock one another down and trample over one another is "highly atypical and is definitely not characteristic of the behavior of panicky persons" (p. 192).

Our conception of panic behavior as presented in Chapter I forces us to take issue with this view. We consider panic behavior to be *only* that flight behavior which is destructive to the group.

THE BEHAVIOR OF PANIC PARTICIPANTS
Enrico L. Quarantelli

Sociologists and social psychologists have long lamented the lack of a systematic set of empirically based generalizations and conceptualizations in the area of crowd behavior. Those activities encompassed by the term "panic" have especially been represented by a very slim body of nonspeculative research and an almost nonexistent set of theoretical propositions. Consequently, it is the aim of this paper to present some general observations based on field data, concerning certain aspects of this form of collective behavior.

Reprinted from *Sociology and Social Research*, 1957, **41**, 187-194, with permission of the publisher and the author.

The Data

In the course of systematic studies of major and minor disasters the NORC Disaster Team,[1] as part of its multioriented project, investigated the phenomena of panic. Team members using tape recorders interviewed approximately 1,000 persons involved in a variety of community-wide and localized disasters— ranging from large-scale explosions, earthquakes, and tornadoes to airplane crashes, hotel and apartment house fires, train wrecks, and asphyxiation incidents. A few of the interviews were conducted within 24 hours of the event, some within several days, but most about a week later. While the recordings varied in length from a quarter of an hour to 4 hours, the average was about an hour and a half. It is from an analysis of these interviews, largely unstructured in form and designed to evoke the freest and fullest expression possible on the part of respondents, that the following observations about panic participants are primarily drawn. This primary source of data was supplemented by carefully evaluated material found in documentary sources dealing with behavior in crisis situations.

Two Conceptions of Panic Participants

In the literature the term "panic" is used to refer to many things. Thus, one finds it applied to such divergent behavior as a single individual's unrealistic

[1] Acknowledgment is made to the National Opinion Research Center, University of Chicago, for permission to use the interview data on which this article is in part based. The research by NORC was undertaken under a contract with the Army Chemical Center, Department of the Army. However, the opinion and conclusions expressed in this article are those of the author and do not necessarily represent the views of NORC, the Army Chemical Center, or the Department of the Army. For a partial summary of the NORC studies see Charles Fritz and Eli Marks, "The NORC Studies of Human Behavior in Disaster," *Journal of Social Issues*, 10 (3rd issue, 1954):26-41.

anxieties to a group's ill-coordinated activities; at times its referent ranges from paralysis of action to a wild outburst of flight. However, the fact that the concept is commonly used in an ambiguous and vague way need not detain us here. Attempts at a conceptual clarification of the varying kinds of socially disorganizing and personally disrupting types of behavior characterized as panic have been presented elsewhere. For our purposes, panic can be conceived of as involving actual (or attempted) physical flight. The term will be used in this sense throughout the paper.

What of the behavior of the participant in this form of flight activity? One conception fairly well dominates the thinking of most individuals who have dealt with the phenomena. At least, a widely accepted image of the panic participant can be discerned. It is that, generally speaking, the panicky person is an individual who has been fairly well divested of all or almost all of his socially acquired characteristics. He is thought of as behaving in a completely irresponsible or antisocial manner, blindly trampling over people in a way analogous, if not completely similar, to the way animals act in a wild and chaotic stampede. The fleeing is visualized as irrational and nonfunctional or maladaptive to the dangerous situation. The uncritically acting participant is conceived as having little awareness of how or why he is running, or often, because of his emotional state of terror, what he is running from.

As Strauss in a broader context has indicated, such a conception of the panic participant implies a "layer-cake version of response organization." [2] In a crisis or

---

[2] Anselm L. Strauss, "Concepts, Communication, and Groups," in Muzafer Sherif and M. O. Wilson (eds.), *Group Relations at the Crossroads* (New York: Harper & Brothers, 1953), p. 107.

emergency situation the veneer of culture or of social living is seen as cast off with the hidden-beast-in-man coming to the fore. In most respects, this conception views the panic participant as one who has lost his humanness, who has been stripped down to sheer emotional reaction, or who has reverted to an animallike level of response.

That this image of panic behavior is commonly held by most sociologists is not surprising, for actually it represents but a logical extension of the supposed behavior of crowd members. The individual in the crowd (especially an acting crowd) is generally characterized as acting irrationally and in an uncontrolled fashion, as responding uncritically to stimulations and suggestions, as interacting on the primitive level of emotional contagion, etc. And since panic is thought of as an extreme form of crowd behavior, it follows that the behavior of panic participants should be thought of as exhibiting in most extreme form the attributed characteristics of individuals in a crowd.

A somewhat different position regarding crowd (and consequently panic) behavior is taken in this paper. The viewpoint here assumed is part of the growing conviction among some students of crowd behavior that the social primitivization usually attributed to the behavior of an individual in a crowd, at the very least, is a vast oversimplification if not actual conceptual distortion of the behavior that occurs. This emerging viewpoint is possibly best summed up in the following quotation which notes that, whatever "eccentric" or "deviant" form human behavior may take, it still is "the result of particular imagery, of particular definitions of situations, of interaction that still involves high order sign behavior, including complex and socialized emoting, perceiving, and remembering." [3] In short, the behavior of crowd members necessarily involves very intricate, socially learned modes of responses.

The behavior of panic participants may be conceived of in a similar way. Whatever else panic behavior may involve, it does represent the behavior of a socialized individual, perceiving and thinking in socially defined and supported ways, reacting to socially interpreted situations, and interacting with and giving meanings to the actions of still other social beings. Therefore, panic behavior must be understood in such terms and not by recourse to an explanation basically involving nonsocial factors.

Aspects of Panic Behavior

On the basis of the aforementioned data, it appears that there are certain aspects of panic behavior. These will now be stated in a series of propositions or hypotheses that may serve as bases for further research.

1. The panic participant perceives a specific threat to physical survival. He defines the panic-producing situation as highly and personally threatening. Whether this is arrived at individually or through interaction with others, the situation is defined as involving a direct threat to one's very physical existence. This is a different experience from that where a threat to the ego may be perceived but where the threat is not conceived of in personal bodily terms (e.g., in becoming bankrupt).

---

[3] Strauss, *op. cit.*, p. 109. His discussion is not specifically directed to crowd behavior. Rather it questions the validity of conceiving human beings as biological organisms upon which layers of social norms have been imposed, with the norms becoming inoperative in time of stress. However, logically extended, this criticism is equally applicable to most conceptions of the behavior of crowd members.

Moreover, the panic participant is aware of what he is afraid *of*. In contrast to the anxiety-stricken person who is unable to label any object in the environment to account for his sense of terror, the panic-stricken person is able to designate the object or event to which he is reacting with fear. Actually, it is only because he can name the threat and localize it in time and space that the panic participant is even able to orient himself so that he can flee. Without a specific object from which an orientation could be taken, physical withdrawal would be an impossibility. An undefined object cannot be perceived as threatening, much less fled from.

2. The panic participant is future-threat rather than past-danger oriented. His attention is focused on what may occur rather than on what has happened. His thinking is not oriented toward such dangers as have already been experienced, but instead is focused on the possibility of becoming blocked off from escaping from an impending threat. Especially salient in his thought is the anticipation of possible entrapment. Furthermore, the threat is perceived as having immediate effects, at most within a time span of several minutes. A rapid reaction of some sort is considered necessary in order to survive the quickly anticipated consequences of the threat.

However, that the panicky individual reacts toward very immediately rising threats rather than retrospective dangers does not mean that there necessarily exists an objective threat. In fact, the realness or illusoriness of the peril is, as far as a panicky reaction is concerned, of little import. Regardless of the objective circumstances, it is how the person defines the situation and is supported in his definition by others that determines his reaction. Thus, panicky reactions will occur in situations involving no real threat simply because a threat is perceived as possible. Similarly, the calmness of people in certain objectively threatening situations frequently stems from a discrepancy between the actual situation and their mutually supporting definition of it as nonthreatening.

3. The panic participant is acutely self-conscious and fearful. In contrast to the reactions involved in the behavior of most crowd members, the panic participant is acutely self-conscious. The more threatening he defines the situation, the greater his awareness of himself. Fear brings with it a sharp visualization of self being threatened.

However, the panicky reaction is characterized not so much by the presence of fear as by unchecked fear. As is illustrated by the behavior of combat soldiers, a person may feel extreme fear for his physical safety and yet maintain a high degree or even complete control over his impulse to flee from the threatening situation. An individual gives overt expression to his fear only if he comes to feel that he (and others that may be with him) are helpless and powerless to cope with the threat. A complete focalization upon the idea of escaping from the immediate area of threat will especially come to the fore if the individual perceives himself as being dependent solely on his own efforts for the attainment of safety.

4. The panic participant is relatively aware of his activities. The focalization of thought on escape accompanied by a loss of control over fear does not mean that a panicky person is completely unresponsive to other objects in the situation or that he just runs in a headlong stampede. On the contrary, a panicky individual orients his fleeing and modifies his behavior in terms of the circumstances he believes are facing him.

Thus, a panic participant does not blindly or randomly run into objects; if possible he goes around obstacles in his path. An attempt is made to go through a door before an attempt is made to flee through a window, etc. Panic flight is directed toward the goal of getting away from the area of danger. The oft-noticed convergence of fleeing persons in a collective panic frequently occurs because individuals, seeing others flee in one direction, assume that escape is possible in that direction.

Sometimes a panicky person may appear to move in the direction of the threat and further endanger himself, e.g., by running toward sheets of flame. However, this is not blind and irrational fleeing as it overtly may appear. Generally what is involved in such instances is that the threatened person believes the only way to safety lies in that direction (e.g., in the belief or knowledge that there is a door behind the flames). The person is thus simply orienting his behavior to the situation as he or others define it for him, perceiving and responding to those elements in the situation which are relevant to his attempt to escape.

Similarly a panicky person does not continue running till physical exhaustion sets in. The characteristically short duration of panic flight to a great extent stems from the fact that the panicky person runs only as long as he conceives of himself as still within the danger area and exposed to the consequences of the threat. To the extent that he or others for him redefine the situation as nonthreatening, the flight immediately ceases.

5. The panic participant is nonrational in his flight behavior. That panic flight involves a degree of awareness on the part of a participant does not mean that it is a highly rational activity in the sense of its involving

the weighing of alternative courses of action that might be followed in the situation. On the other hand, the thinking of the panicky person is not "irrational" if by that is meant anything in the way of faulty or illogical deductions from given premises. From the position of an observer with a much broader perspective of the total situation, this may appear to be the case. However, from a participant's viewpoint, given his necessarily more limited perspective of only certain portions of all the circumstances involved, no such interpretation of irrationality is warranted. To the panicky person, his flight appears to him quite appropriate to the situation as he perceives and defines it at that time, however he may retrospectively evaluate it.

Rather than being rational or irrational, the behavior of a panic participant is nonrational. In the face of an immediate possibility of personal annihilation, the potential courses of action available range from direct individual or collective attack to movement away from the endangering object. The panicky person, thinking only of escaping, makes no overt attempt to cope directly with the threat other than to flee from it. He does not engage in other activity designed to bring the threat under control. The panic participant is nonrational, not because of a failure to think or because of illogical thinking, but simply because of the extreme focalization of his thought and consequent overt activity to remove himself from the threatening area.

6. The panic participant's flight is not necessarily nonfunctional or maladaptive. Because a panicky reaction is nonrational, it is not always nor necessarily personally and collectively inappropriate to the situation.

That a panicky person flees and makes no direct at-

tempt to cope with the threat does not make his behavior necessarily nonfunctional. Frequently, running
away is the most adaptive course of action that the
person could take in the particular situation. Thus, to
flee from a building where the ceiling is threatening to
collapse as a result of earthquake shocks, is on most
occasions the most appropriate behavior possible. In
such instances the flight is functional, if functionality
under such circumstances is thought of as behavior
which from an over-all viewpoint is appropriate to the
maintenance of the life of a threatened individual.

Likewise, the panicky person's behavior is not necessarily collectively maladaptive. There are many occasions where flight simultaneously engaged in by a
number of persons not only is individually functional
but also has no inappropriate social consequences.
People can run out of houses without having any or
very little bodily contact of a destructive sort with one
another. In fact, it is only very rarely, and almost always because of the presence of physical barriers, that
panicky individuals may proceed to knock one another
down and to trample over each other. Such collectively
maladaptive activity, however, is highly atypical and
is definitely not characteristic of the behavior of
panicky persons.

The conception of panic flight as being nonfunctional or maladaptive actually conceals a hindsight
normative judgment which cannot be considered here.
Suffice it to say that panic behavior sometimes (and
more often) is functional and adaptive and sometimes
it is not. If the latter, it is generally so because of
specific physical circumstances that prevent individuals from fleeing unhampered or unhampering others.

7. The panic participant acts in a nonsocial manner
in his flight behavior. The panicky person acts in a

nonsocial way in that he disregards the usual social relationships and interaction patterns that guide behavior. Even the strongest primary group ties may be shattered and the most socially expected behavior patterns ignored. Thus, a panicky mother may run out and leave her child in a house that she thinks is going to explode.

The panicky person is very highly self-centered, thinking only of saving himself. In this sense, panic flight represents very highly individualistic behavior. It involves completely individual as over against collective activity in reacting to the problem of escaping from a threat. In its total absence of concerted group action, panic behavior thus represents nonsocial behavior at its zenith.

This nonsocial aspect may be short lived, but it is one of the major characteristics which distinguish panic flight from nonpanic withdrawal behavior. In the case of nonpanic withdrawal, confused and ill-coordinated activity may be manifested, but the conventional social roles and the normal interactional patterns are not totally disregarded. Thus, when a plane hit an apartment house in one disaster, most families evacuated as units, neighbors were warned, alternative courses of action were discussed, etc. People acted in an erratic and partially unorganized fashion, but, unlike when people are panicky, most of their behavior was in terms of the group norms that ordinarily guided their activities. Such excited flight is only superficially similar to panic flight.

In stating that the panicky reaction is nonsocial, there is no implication that the panic participant regresses to infantile reaction patterns or reverts to purely reflexive or biologically given ways of reacting. That is not so. Learned motor patterns of action are not forgotten by the panicky individual. Thus, in certain situations where it is physically possible, the panicky person may manifest flight by driving vehicles, swimming, digging, riding horses, etc. He maintains the learned neuromuscular coordinations effective for the carrying out of complex motor activities, as well as the capacity for perceiving, remembering, thinking, etc., in socially learned ways as was indicated earlier. The nonsocial aspect of the panicky reaction is primarily in regard to failures to play conventional social roles and to follow the expected interactional patterns.

Social Interaction

The utmost importance of the nature of the interaction that occurs prior to and during panic flight should be especially stressed. In the case of collective panics, it is through individuals interacting with one another that there occurs a cognitive clarification of what the situation is and what can or cannot be done about it. Social interaction is basic in bringing about the definition of the crisis situation as a threatening one. It plays a major part in reinforcing the definition of the situation as one in which only flight is possible. Finally, panic flight frequently terminates as a result of the interaction among the participants, leading them to perceive themselves as out of the danger area. And possibly most important of all, it is frequently the presence and response of other persons that motivates individuals to control their fears, consequently diminishing the possibility of panicky reactions.

Conclusion

The behavior of panic participants does not represent a primitivization of responses. The panicky reaction is an attempt to adjust to an unexpected and action-demanding circumstance by nonrational and nonsocial individualistic flight. Such behavior nevertheless is, in terms of an earlier quotation, "the result of particular imagery, of particular definitions of situations, of interaction that still involves high order sign behavior,[4] including complex and socialized emoting, perceiving, and remembering." The seven propositions advanced in this paper represent an attempt to illustrate this fact—that a once socialized person even under extreme stress does not regress to the "brute level," but rather shifts to an individualistic solution of the crisis while continuing to use socially learned modes of responses in the process.

---

[4] Strauss, *ibid.*

V

Experimental Approach to Panic Behavior

DISCUSSION

THE EXPERIMENTAL APPROACH

As discussed in Chapter I, panic is one aspect of group behavior which does not permit rigid, precise control to the degree we normally associate with experimental research in psychology. And certainly it would seem less than desirable to attempt to reproduce actual panic conditions in the laboratory. Just such an attempt has been made, however, by J. R. P. French, Jr. (1944), who simulated a fire in a locked room containing the subjects. Beyond the potential danger to the subjects, this method presents methodological difficulties as it is lacking in systematic controls and yields results which are difficult to express in quantitative terms.

A much more fruitful approach to the study of panic behavior would seem to be simulation of the sort used by Alexander Mintz in the article which follows. In this instance, a situation was utilized which was competitive for the subjects; there being a reward and fine system. It simulated a social interaction situation in which cooperative and adaptive behavior on the part of each subject was required in order for him to avoid "losing," that is, paying a fine. Nonadaptive behavior on the part of the subjects could (and did in many groups) lead to a situation in which the majority or all of the subjects would be fined.

The analogy Mintz draws between his experimental arrangement and a theater fire would seem to be appropriate. In such a fire, everyone (or at least most) stands a chance of surviving if all cooperate and file out in an orderly manner. If the behavior is not cooperative and orderly, and leads to jamming and blocking of the exits (as occurred in the Iroquois Theater and Coconut Grove Fires), fewer of the members stand a chance of surviving.

The demonstration by Mintz that the same nonadaptive behavior often occurring in a theater fire was obtained in his laboratory situation, where the only threat to the individual was a small fine, is extremely significant. Indeed, his approach would seem to offer an excellent vehicle for further research on panic, allowing as it does for quantitative measures of the dependent variable to be provided, as well as the opportunity to experimentally manipulate a wide range of independent variables.

Since it is manifestly impossible to arrange real-life panic situations, as the Germans were reported to have done (Farago, 1942), experimental simulation provides the only opportunity to submit theories of panic to empirical test.

NON-ADAPTIVE GROUP BEHAVIOR
Alexander Mintz

Theoretical Considerations

It is common knowledge that groups of people frequently behave in a way which leads to disastrous
consequences not desired or anticipated by the members of the group. At theater fires, people often block
the exits by pushing, so that individuals are burned or
trampled. Since it normally takes only a few minutes
for a theater to be emptied the strikingly non-adaptive
character of this behavior is obvious.

In the explanations for the occurrence of such behavior offered by social psychologists, intense emotional excitement resulting from mutual facilitation
(or "contagion" or "suggestion") and leading to interference with thinking, adaptive behavior, and the
operation of moral codes, has tended to be viewed as
the decisive factor. Explanations of this general type
can be found in numerous textbooks on social psychology, from that by Ross (21) to those by Britt (3),
Vaughn (27), and Young (31). Ultimately they stem
from the theories of the nature of crowd behavior of
Le Bon (12), who has been an extremely influential
figure in the thinking on social issues of the past fifty
years. He has been an important ideological ancestor
of fascism[1] and nazism; thus Hitler's ideas on social

Reprinted from the *Journal of Abnormal and Social Psychology*, 1951,
46, 150-159, by permission of the American Psychological Association
and the author.

[1] In his last book, Le Bon (13) quotes an interview with Mussolini in
which the latter stated that he read *The Crowd* many times and that
he often refers to it.

psychology as expressed in *Mein Kampf* closely resemble those of Le Bon. Le Bon's theories embodied features which were severely criticized by a number of psychologists. In speaking of emotional interaction between members of a group leading to personality alterations, he postulated the emergence of a group mind based on collective racial unconscious tendencies. These notions of a group mind and racial unconscious were rejected by most psychologists. Nevertheless, his critics often accepted the more essential features of his theory, and crowd membership is often viewed as having an essentially brutalizing effect on people as a result of allegedly regressive, non-adaptive consequences of intense emotion generated by social facilitation.

The explanations of the non-adaptive behavior in panics in terms of emotional excitement are related to a tendency still prevalent in modern psychology to view all emotion as essentially superfluous and even harmful. For a number of years, many textbooks defined emotion as "disorganized response" and the like. In some textbooks, emotion was treated mainly as something to be controlled. Until quite recently, many books of child rearing contained advice designed to weaken the emotional intimacy between parent and child (28). Actually, a distrust of emotion has been endemic in Western thought ever since the days of Stoic philosophy. In recent years, however, another point of view has tended to emerge. The desirable features of emotional spontaneity have been emphasized by many psychotherapists for a number of years and there are psychoanalysts who characterize the cure in psychotherapy as a process of emotional liberation. More recently, the notion that emotion is essentially non-adaptive has been severely criticized in theoretical psychology (14), and a lively controversy about the question appears to be in progress.

Material will be presented in this paper suggesting that violent emotional excitement is not the decisive factor[2] in the non-adaptive behavior of people in panics and related situations. Instead, it appears to be possible to explain the non-adaptive character of such behavior in terms of their perception of the situation and their expectation of what is likely to happen. In recent times, a number of psychologists have tended to interpret features of human behavior in terms of the phenomenal properties of the situation in which it occurs. Thus Katona reported several studies of the role of the economic situation as experienced by consumers and of their expectations in their economic behavior (7, 8). S. Asch and others explained the effects on value judgment, commonly attributed to prestige suggestion, in terms of the additional cognitive background of the material to be judged provided by the supposedly prestige-loaded items (1, 2). G. Murphy (19) attempted to make the behavior of a foreign government understandable in terms of the political situation as it must be perceived by its members. Wertheimer (29) and his collaborator, E. Levy (15), discussed a number of cases of mental disorder as understandable in terms of the phenomenal properties of their phenomenal environment. As a general postulate, the congruence between the organization of our perception, thought, and expectation on one hand, and our motivation, valuation, and action on the other hand, has been discussed extensively by Koffka (10), Tolman (26), Rogers, Snygg and Combs (25), Cantril (4), Lewin (17), Krech and Crutchfield (11), and others. The theoretical approaches just mentioned are

---

[2] Its existence is not denied.

by no means entirely identical; in some of them the role of ego factors and action potentialities is stressed more than in others (e.g., by Cantril as contrasted with the Gestalt group), but in all of them behavior is viewed as understandable in terms of the phenomenal world.

What are the reasonable expectations of people at a theater fire or in similar circumstances in which a panic is apt to develop? Situations of this type tend to have a characteristically unstable reward structure, which has been generally overlooked by social scientists as a factor in panics. Cooperative behavior is required for the common good but has very different consequences for the individual depending on the behavior of others. Thus at a theater fire, if everyone leaves in an orderly manner, everybody is safe, and an individual waiting for his turn is not sacrificing his interests. But, if the cooperative pattern of behavior is disturbed, the usual advice, "Keep your head, don't push, wait for your turn, and you will be safe," ceases to be valid. If the exits are blocked, the person following this advice is likely to be burned to death. In other words, if everybody cooperates, there is no conflict between the needs of the individual and those of the group. However, the situation changes completely as soon as a minority of people cease to cooperate. A conflict between the needs of the group and the selfish needs of the individual then arises. An individual who recognizes this state of things and who wants to benefit the group must sacrifice his own selfish needs.

It is suggested here that it is chiefly the reward structure of the situations which is responsible for non-adaptive behavior of groups at theater fires and similar situations. People are likely to recognize the threats to themselves, as they appear, and behave accordingly. These situations may be compared to states of unstable equilibrium in mechanics; a cone balanced on its tip is not likely to remain in this position a long time because a slight initial displacement of its center of gravity allows the force of gravity to make it fall all the way. Similarly, cooperative behavior at a theater fire is likely to deteriorate progressively as soon as an initial disturbance occurs. If a few individuals begin to push, the others are apt to recognize that their interests are threatened; they can expect to win through to their individual rewards only by pressing their personal advantages at the group's expense. Many of them react accordingly, a vicious circle is set up, and the disturbance spreads. Competitive behavior (pushing and fighting) may result, as e.g., at theater fires, or the group may disperse as in military panics. There is another factor which makes for further disintegration. As the behavior of the group becomes increasingly disorderly, the amount of noise is apt to increase, and communication may then become so difficult that no plan for restoring order can emerge.

This interpretation is almost the reverse of the conventional ones which ascribe non-adaptive group behavior to emotional facilitation and to the supposed alterations of personality in group situations.

The existence of mutual emotional facilitation is not denied; its operation can be readily observed, e.g., in college students during final examinations, in audiences at sports events, etc. However, it is not believed that emotional excitement as such is responsible for non-adaptive group behavior. There are many situations in which intense emotional excitement is the rule, and yet no non-adaptive group behavior appears. Thus it has been reported that intense fear is practically universally present in soldiers about to go into battle and yet no panic need develop. Similarly, participants in an athletic contest are apt to be so emotionally excited that vomiting is common; no markedly non-adaptive group behavior appears to develop as a result of this kind of intense excitement.

The assumption of personality alterations of people due to crowd membership appears to be entirely unsubstantiated in the case of panics. On the contrary, the competitive behavior or dispersal occurring in panics suggests that group cohesion disappears and that people begin to behave purely as individuals in accordance with their selfish needs.[3] Rather similarly Freud has explained certain types of panics in terms of the disappearance of the libidinal ties between individuals (5, pp. 45-48).

As a first step towards the verification of the proposed theory, a set of laboratory experiments was devised. It was thought that if the theory is correct it should be possible to illustrate its functioning in the laboratory. If not substantiated by laboratory findings, the theory would have to be discarded.

Experimental Design

The experiments were conducted with groups of people, 15 to 21 subjects in each group. The subjects had the task of pulling cones out of a glass bottle; each subject was given a piece of string to which a cone was attached. Cooperation on the part of the subjects was required if the cones were to come out; the physical setup made it easy for "traffic jams" of cones to appear at the bottle neck. Only one cone could come out at a time; even a near-tie between two cones at the bottle neck prevented both from coming

---

[3] The writer is indebted to Dr. M. Scheerer for pointing out this inference from the suggested theory.

out because the narrow apex of the second cone, wedged into the bottle neck, blocked the path for the wide base of the cone ahead of it. The cones had to arrive at the bottle neck in order, one at a time.

Experimental Situations—1. One of the experimental setups was designed to show that it was possible to produce disorganized, uncooperative, non-adaptive group behavior resulting in "traffic jams" by duplicating the essential features of panic-producing situations, as explained in the theoretical section of this paper. The experimental situation was represented to the subjects as a game in which each participant could win or lose money. A subject could win or lose depending on how successful he was in pulling out his cone. Success was defined in terms of arbitrary time limits in some experiments. In other experiments water was made to flow into the bottle through a spout near the bottom and the subject was successful if his cone came out of the bottle untouched by the water. Inasmuch as the rewards and fines were offered to individuals, depending on what would happen to their particular cones, it was thought that the cooperative pattern of behavior, required for group success, would be easily disrupted; a momentary "traffic jam" at the bottle neck would be perceived by some of the subjects as threatening them with loss in the game as a result of the anticipated failure of cooperative behavior. These subjects would be tempted to save themselves from the loss by pulling out of turn. Some of them would probably do so, and thus the situation could be expected rapidly to deteriorate after an initial disturbance occurred.

In order that subjects who recognized that full success was out of their reach should not stop trying, intermediate steps between full success and full failure were announced. The details and the amounts of rewards and fines are summarized in the table of results.[4] The monetary rewards and fines were very small, the rewards for full success ranging from 10 to 25 cents, the fines for full failure from 1 to 10 cents. The very small fines were decided upon because it was intended to show that the characteristically inefficient, non-adaptive features of group behavior such as occurs in panics can be reproduced in a situation in which there was no opportunity for fear. It was not thought that the small rewards and fines were likely to constitute real financial incentives for college students. They were introduced so as to emphasize the nature of the experimental situation as a game in which individuals could win or lose.

2. In the contrasting experimental setups there were no individual rewards or fines, and there was no flow of water except for a few control experiments. The experiments were described as attempts to measure the ability of groups of people to behave cooperatively. Good performances of other groups were quoted. It was expected that under these conditions no "traffic jams" would develop. Subjects had no motivation to disregard any plan that might be devised by the group; the only incentive offered was membership in a group of people who were going to

[4] The appendix, including a detailed table of the data from each experiment, has been deposited with the American Documentation Institute to reduce printing costs. For the six pages of the appendix, order Document 2815 from American Documentation Institute, 1719 N Street, N.W., Washington 6, D.C., remitting $0.50 for microfilm (images 1 inch high on standard 35 mm. motion picture film) or $0.60 for photocopies (6 x 8 inches) readable without optical aid.

show their ability to cooperate effectively with each other.[5] Thus the reward structure was the principal experimental variable studied in these two experimental situations.

3. Another variable investigated was the excitement built up by mutual facilitation. In a number of "no-reward" experiments several subjects were asked to act as accomplices. They were secretly instructed before the experiment began to scream, behave excitedly, swear, and make as much noise as possible. To limit their influence to emotional facilitation they were asked not to give specific bad advice nor to disturb the workings of any plan the group might decide upon. It was expected that the added emotional excitement, which is the major factor in Le Bon's and similar theories of panics, would not have much effect on the results.

4. In certain of the reward-and-fine experiments an attempt was made to minimize the opportunities for mutual emotional facilitation by largely preventing the subjects from seeing each other. This was accomplished by a circular screen with holes for eyes and arms and with vertical partitions on the outside, placed around the glass bottle. Each subject stood in an individual "stall" hiding him from his neighbors; he saw the bottle standing on the floor through the eye hole; only his arm and eyes could be seen by the other subjects, and the eyes were not likely to be seen because the subjects were mainly looking at the bottle tied to the floor. In order to prevent excited screams, the subjects were asked to remain silent after the experiment began, which request was largely complied

---

[5] The need to belong has been particularly emphasized as an important motive, among others, by E. Fromm (6) and M. Sherif (22). The important role which group membership plays in industry has been investigated particularly in the Hawthorne studies (e.g., 30).

with. It was expected that the results would be essentially the same as those in the other reward-and-fine experiments.

5. A third variable which was introduced in a few of the experiments was interference with the opportunity to arrive at a plan of action. In most of the experiments the subjects were not prevented from conducting preliminary discussions; in almost all instances either they started such a discussion immediately or asked for permission to do so, which was given. Only twice did a group fail to discuss and agree upon a plan when discussion was not explicitly forbidden. On the other hand, in two of the reward-and-fine experiments conducted early in the study the subjects were forbidden to talk to each other both before and during the experiment; in one reward-and-fine experiment conducted immediately after three no-reward experiments with the same group, the subjects were prevented from having a preliminary discussion so that no plan could be agreed upon beforehand, but were allowed to talk during the experiment.

Apparatus and Procedure—Figure 1 gives the shapes and dimensions of the cones and of the bottle and shows where the pieces of string were attached. The cones were made of wood in the early experiments. Later, aluminum cones were substituted [6] because the wooden one tended to become tightly forced into the bottle neck and had to be loosened by hand (which was done promptly by the experimenter). In the experiments with the aluminum cones the glass bottle had too large an opening, which was remedied by the insertion of a cylinder with a 1-inch hole bored through it. This cylinder, made of aluminum, had rub-

---

[6] Post-war shortages prevented the use of smooth plastic material, as had been intended.

ber tape wound on the outside. It was forced tightly into the bottle neck and was tied down with wire. In addition to cutting down the opening of the bottle to the desired diameter, it also protected the glass from the impact of the aluminum cones. A sponge rubber

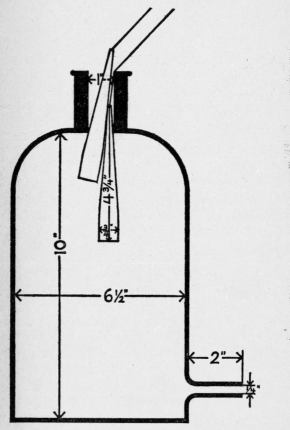

FIG. 1. *Cross-Section of the Glass Bottle with Two Cones Shown Blocking the Bottle Neck*
MAIN DIMENSIONS OF THE EQUIPMENT ARE GIVEN.

pad was cemented to the bottom of the glass bottle. A rubber tube could be attached to the spout and lead either to a water faucet or to another similar bottle placed high up.

The screen was made of corrugated cardboard. Two strips 23.5 feet in length were cut off a 3-foot-wide roll and glued together, so that a strip 6 feet wide resulted. The ends of the strip could be brought together and the strip could be made to stand on edge in the shape of a cylinder around the bottle. Pieces of corrugated cardboard, 3 feet by 1 foot, were attached to the screen at intervals of 1 foot 3 inches, subdividing the space immediately around the screen into individual stalls. The rectangular eye holes cut in each stall were 1.5 inches high, 5 inches wide; their bottom was 4 feet 8 inches above the ground; the roughly circular arm holes were about 5 inches in diameter and 3 feet 1.5 inches from the ground, near the right hand edges of the stalls. There were 18 stalls altogether.

In putting the cones into the bottle, care was taken to prevent the tangling of strings; as an added precaution, the fishing line used as string was waxed in later experiments. In the early experiments the bottle was tied to the legs of a table on which it was placed. In the later experiments it was placed on the floor and tied to nails driven into the floor like tent stakes.

The instructions were not rigidly standardized. The rewards were always larger than the fines, ranging from 10 to 25 cents in different experiments. The fines ranged from 1 to 5 cents. Examples of the two main types of instructions and other details of the experimental procedures follow:

1. *A Reward-and-Fine Experiment.* "I need volunteers for an experiment which is set up as a game in

which you can win up to a quarter or lose up to 2 cents [or 5 or 10 cents as the case may have been]." Then, after the volunteers (sometimes after some urging) assembled: "As I said, this is going to be like a game. Each of you will receive a cone with an attached piece of string. All cones will be placed into the bottle. The object of the game is to get your cone out before it gets wet. You may start pulling when I give the signal, 'ready-go!' but only one cone can come out at a time. If two get into the bottle neck, neither comes out (demonstration). Simultaneously, I shall start water flowing into the bottle. If your cone comes out dry you get a quarter. If less than a third of it is wet, you get nothing; if more than a third but less than two-thirds of it gets wet, you pay a penny fine. If the cone is more than two-thirds wet, you pay a two-cent fine. The fines will be contributed to the Student Council." Then the students were asked to put their cones in the bottle. While they were doing it, a discussion of a plan for action generally started and was not interfered with by the experimenter.

The signal to begin was given after an agreement was reached by the subjects. When in doubt, the experimenter asked the group whether they were ready.

2. *A No-Reward Experiment.* "This is going to be an experiment in which your ability to cooperate with each other will be measured. I need volunteers." Then, after the subjects assembled around the bottle, the procedure continued exactly as in the reward-and-fine experiments except that no rewards were offered, the rubber tube was not attached, and no reference to water was made. Instead, after the possibility of "traffic jams" was demonstrated, the experimenter said: "In spite of the smallness of the opening, a group of students from the University of Nevada succeeded in cooperating with each other so well that they got all their cones out in 10.5 seconds. See if you can do as well as the Westerners!"

Results

The conditions and results of all of the experiments conducted so far are indicated in a table in an appendix.[7] Forty-two experiments with 26 groups of subjects were performed altogether, including some preliminary and control experiments conducted to investigate potential sources of error. In the table each experiment is identified by a code symbol consisting of letters and a number.

One experiment (R1) was conducted before the procedure was fully developed; there were no fines and only one reward level was announced. No "traffic jam" resulted.

There were 16 experiments with rewards and fines. In three of them (RF1 to RF3) discussion was interfered with before the experiment, so that the subjects had no opportunity to devise a plan of action. In all three experiments "traffic jams" developed. In only one of them did the subjects succeed in pulling *any* cones out of the bottle—two cones out of 19 in 40 seconds; these same subjects had successfully pulled out *all* cones in 18.6 seconds and 23 seconds in two immediately preceding trials in which there had been no rewards and in which they had had the opportunity to agree upon a plan of action.

In the other 13 reward-and-fine experiments (RF4 to RF16) discussion was not interfered with. In eight of these experiments (RF4 to RF6, RF9, RF10, RF12, RF13, and RF16) there were serious "traffic jams," the large majority of the cones failing to be pulled out of the bottle within times ranging from one to approximately two minutes. In another experiment almost half of the cones were in the bottle after 1

---

[7] See footnote 4, above.

minute (RF15). In two of these experiments (RF15 and RF16) the factor of mutual emotional facilitation was minimized by the use of the screen. The results were much the same as in most of the other reward-and-fine experiments, suggesting that this factor was not primarily responsible for the results.

In four of the reward-and-fine experiments (RF7, RF8, RF11, RF14) there were no serious "traffic jams"; all or almost all of the cones came out of the bottle in less than a minute. In three of these experiments the experimenter was unable to persuade the winners to take the rewards; apparently the subjects had failed to accept the situation as a game with winners and losers. In one of these experiments there was an additional factor which probably interfered with "traffic jams"; immediately before this experiment (RF14) these subjects had participated in another (NR5) in which no rewards had been offered and in which the fastest time of any group was achieved (10 seconds). The subjects knew the time of this trial; the time allowance for winning exceeded it by 5 seconds, so that the chances of losing must have been recognized as slight by the subjects.

In the remaining 25 experiments there were no rewards or fines. Twenty of these experiments were described to the subjects as measures of cooperation. These experiments fell into three groups. Experiments NR1 to NR5 were conducted with groups of subjects who had not been previously exposed to similar experiments, and under "natural" conditions, i.e., without the experimenter entering into a conspiracy with accomplices. Experiments NR6 to NR12 were similar but were conducted immediately after experiments with accomplices. Experiments ANR1 to ANR8 were the experiments with accomplices who had been instructed to make noise and to stir up excitement in the group.

No serious "traffic jam" developed in any of these experiments, not in those with new subjects, nor in those with accomplices, nor in those preceded by experiments with accomplices. The times for taking *all* cones out of the bottle ranged in these three groups of experiments from 10 to 22 seconds, from 10.5 to 30 seconds and from 13.4 to 59 seconds.

The experimenter's accomplices were generally able to stir up excitement but this excitement failed to disrupt the cooperative behavior of the group to an extent comparable to that of the effect of the individual rewards and fines. In most of the reward-and-fine experiments the majority of the cones were still in the bottle after a minute or longer had elapsed.

Did the accomplices have any effect? The mean times of the two groups of the no-reward, no-accomplice experiments were 16.8 seconds (NR1 to NR5) and 19.6 seconds (NR6 to NR12); the mean time of the accomplice experiments was 34.4 seconds. The difference between the times of the two groups of experiments without accomplices is very small and not statistically significant. In the accomplice experiments the mean time was longer, significantly so at the .01 level of confidence, suggesting that the accomplices did have some disrupting effect. However, a closer examination of the data shows that the two longest times in the accomplice experiments were obtained when some of the accomplices had misunderstood the instructions and gave bad advice to the group. If the results of these two experiments (ANR1 and ANR8) are eliminated, the mean time drops to 26.4 seconds, and the critical ratio (Fisher's *t* for small, uncorrelated samples) indicates that the difference between this time and that of the no-accomplice experiments is too small to reach the conventional standards of statistical significance ($t = 1.82$, $d.f. = 16$, $P > .05$). Thus it was not established with certainty that the accomplices who made noise and stirred up excitement without giving bad advice had a disrupting effect on group cooperation. They may have had; the evidence was inconclusive. More experiments would have been needed to establish this point. The experiments with accomplices were designed merely to discover whether an additional opportunity for mutual emotional facilitation would seriously disrupt group cooperation. They served their purpose in showing that it did not; and since the question whether it had a minor disrupting effect was not directly related to the main problem of this study in any case, the matter was not further investigated.

There were several additional no-reward experiments (PC1 to PC5). One of these was described to the subjects as a preliminary trial conducted in order to determine the proper conditions for the next experiment in which rewards were to be offered. This was the only no-reward experiment in which a serious "traffic jam" developed; there was no organized plan for action in this group, probably because the subjects were not sufficiently motivated to devise one before the experiment began. The remaining four experiments were described to the subjects, who had previously participated in reward-and-fine experiments, as control experiments conducted in order to demonstrate to the group what were the effects of the rewards. In view of the common claim of the subjects that the flow of water was primarily responsible for the "traffic jams" water was made to flow in three of them. No serious "traffic jam" developed in any of the control experiments. On the other hand, three out of the four times were distinctly slow ones as compared to those in the other no-reward experiments. It is not clear whether this finding was due to fluctuations of random sampling ("chance"), whether the subjects were inadequately motivated in these "control" experiments, or whether the earlier reward-and-fine experiments had continued bad effects on the cooperative behavior of the subjects. The matter was not investigated at this time.

After each experiment or group of experiments the subjects were told by the experimenter about the true nature of the experiments and about the results obtained so far. The explanations were followed by discussions. In the groups which had failed to pull out the cones from the bottle, marked tendencies towards rationalization appeared during these discussions. Subjects tended to explain the bad results of their group in terms of supposedly tangled strings, effects of the water, or insufficient time for the formulation of a plan, disregarding the fact that these factors failed to produce "traffic jams" in no-reward experiments.

Discussion

The theory presented at the beginning of this paper is opposed to the common tendency to view emotion as a predominantly disruptive factor in behavior. It developed out of an attempt to reconstruct the phenomenal situation in circumstances leading to a panic. The present writer views this approach as a fruitful one and finds it congenial. On the other hand, it is not considered to be the only fruitful approach to psychology and the experiments reported in this paper do not constitute a crucial test of this type of approach. One can treat the same situation and behavior occurring in it in phenomenal terms (25), or in terms of psychological "genotypical" constructs (17), or in physiological terms, or in terms of stimuli, responses, and operants which are not defined physiologically (24). In other words, one can operate within any one of several possible universes of discourse. One such universe of discourse may be more convenient and more suggestive of fruitful hypotheses to a particular investigator, than another, and one universe of discourse may have philosophical advantages compared to another one. Generally speaking, the choice of the universe of discourse cannot be definitely settled by any experiments. Personal preferences of investigators vary, and facts tend to be equally compatible with virtually all philosophical systems except possibly in very advanced sciences.[8]

The experiments provide laboratory demonstrations for our hypothesis and partially verify the hypothesis. The behavior of the subjects did not tend towards inefficiency unless the reward structure of the situation provided them with incentives to behave uncooperatively after the cooperative pattern of group behavior was disturbed. There were no "traffic jams" in the no-reward experiments. Emotional excitement produced by the experimenter's accomplices interfered with the efficiency of group behavior only to a minor extent, if at all, compared to the effects of individual rewards and fines. On the other hand, there were inefficient behavior and "traffic jams" in more than half of the reward-and-fine experiments, in which the subjects were confronted with the probability of individual failure, as soon as the bottle neck was temporarily blocked.

---

[8] The author hopes to develop this viewpoint in another paper. The ideas expressed here have been influenced by the epistemological considerations of H. Reichenbach in one of his earlier works (20).

This result was obtained without any more serious threat to the individuals than the loss of ten cents at most and probably a mild feeling of failure in a game. Thus intense fear was not found to be an essential condition of chaotic, non-adaptive group behavior analogous to that occurring in panics.

"Traffic jams" did not occur in all of the reward-and-fine experiments and were not expected to. In an experiment with 15 to 20 subjects one cannot be certain that one or a few subjects will create a disturbance within the short time available. With larger groups the percentage of "traffic jams" should be larger; the more people there are, the more likely it becomes that one uncooperative individual will create the initial disturbance which leads to deterioration of the situation.

The theory presented here, if correct, appears to apply to many situations and to contribute to the understanding of a number of social and economic phenomena. Situations with reward structures resembling that of panics and the reward-and-fine experiments reported here seem to be numerous. Tendencies towards non-adaptive group behavior are clearly present in many such situations, regardless of the presence or absence of face-to-face contacts between people and opportunities for mutual emotional facilitation. Runs on banks resulting in bank failures, violations of price-fixing agreements among business men resulting in cut-throat competition, hoarding behavior of consumers during periods of scarcity of goods resulting in shortages are all forms of ultimately non-adaptive behavior which can be interpreted in terms of unstable reward structures of the situations. On the other hand, there are situations in which the appearance of danger does not provide incentives for anti-social behavior. In such situations no chaotic non-adaptive behavior of groups seems to occur in spite of the catastrophic nature of the danger and ample opportunity for face-to-face contacts. There seem to be no panics when people are trapped so that there can be no struggle for an exit, e.g., at submarine and mine disasters (32).

It is intended to deal in future publications with social and economic data pertaining to both group behavior which tends to deteriorate and group behavior which tends to remain adaptive in nature. Full verification of the theory cannot be accomplished in terms of laboratory experiments; it requires investigation of real life situations. An examination of one set of relevant data, viz., gasoline consumption figures during the period of developing gasoline shortages in 1941, is in progress at present.

The experiments reported here belong also in a second theoretical context. In these experiments a system of individual rewards resulted in strikingly inefficient behavior, while the goal of demonstrating the ability of the group to cooperate produced much more orderly action. These findings may be compared with those of the type reported by Maller (18) and Sims (23), who found that individual competition led to greater efficiency than group competition. It should be noted that the structure of the tasks in these earlier experiments and those reported here differed. In the former experiments the subjects worked separately and could not interfere with each other as readily as in our experiments. Thus the experiments provide an additional illustration for the caution that any generalization pertaining to the effect of competition on behavior is limited not only by the prevalent social norms and personality characteristics, but also by the nature of the task, as was pointed out, e.g., by Klineberg (9, p. 338).

Summary

A theory is suggested, explaining the non-adaptive features of behavior occurring in panics in terms of the reward structure of the situations rather than in terms of mutual facilitation of emotion. In panic-producing situations cooperative behavior is needed for success and is rewarding to individuals as long as everybody cooperates. However, once the cooperative pattern of behavior is disturbed, cooperation ceases to be rewarding to the individuals; then a competitive situation is apt to develop which may lead to disaster. Thus at a theater fire it pays not to push if everybody cooperates, but if a few uncooperative individuals block the exits by pushing, then any individual who does not push can expect that he will be burned. Pushing becomes the advantageous (or least disadvantageous) form of behavior for individuals, and disorder leading to disastrous consequences spreads rapidly.

Laboratory experiments with miniature social situations are reported in which the effects of the reward structure on group behavior in situations in which cooperation was required for success was studied. In these experiments the subjects had to take cones out of a bottle; only one cone could be taken out at a time and the bottle neck was easily blocked by too many cones arriving simultaneously, so that the cones came out only if the subjects cooperated with each other. The situation was represented to some of the groups of subjects as a game in which one could win or lose small sums of money; to other groups the experiment was described as a measure of their ability to cooperate. The opportunities for mutual emotional facilitation were also varied in some experiments.

In the majority of cases, serious "traffic jams" resulted when individual rewards and fines were offered, preventing the taking out of any or most of the cones. No similar disturbances were observed in the "measure of cooperativeness" experiments. In the reward-and-fine experiments, the introduction of a screen hiding the subjects from each other, so as to minimize opportunities for mutual emotional facilitation, did not prevent "traffic jams" from occurring. In the experiments without individual rewards, excited screaming in the group (arranged by the experimenter) had little if any effect on the results.

The experiments gave the expected results, thus contributing to a partial verification of the theory; full verification would require examination of real life data, which is planned. The theory appears to apply to other social phenomena in addition to panic.

References

1. Asch, S. E. Understanding vs. suggestion in the social field. *Psychol. Bull.*, 1940, 39, 466-467.
2. Asch, S. E. The doctrines of suggestion, prestige and imitation in social psychology. *Psychol. Rev.*, 1948, 55, 250-276.
3. Britt, S. H. *Social psychology of modern life*. New York: Farrar and Rinehart, 1941.
4. Cantril, H. *Understanding man's social behavior, preliminary notes*. Princeton: Office of Public Opinion Research, 1947.
5. Freud, S. *Group psychology and analysis of the ego*. London: Hogarth Press, 1910.
6. Fromm, E. *Escape from freedom*. New York: Farrar and Rinehart, 1941.
7. Katona, G. *War without inflation*. New York: Columbia Univ. Press, 1942.
8. Katona, G. Expectations and buying intentions of consumers. *Amer. Psychologist,* 1948, 3, 273.

9. KLINEBERG, O. *Social psychology*. New York: Holt, 1940.
10. KOFFKA, K. *Principles of gestalt psychology*. New York: Harcourt, Brace, 1935.
11. KRECH, D., and CRUTCHFIELD, R. C. *Theory and problems of social psychology*. New York: McGraw-Hill, 1948.
12. LE BON, G. *The crowd*. London: Unwin, 1916.
13. LE BON, G. *Bases scientifiques d'une philosophie de l'histoire*. Paris: Flammarion, 1931.
14. LEEPER, R. W. A motivational theory of emotion to replace "emotion as disorganized response." *Psychol. Rev.*, 1948, 55, 5-21.
15. LEVY, E. A case of mania with its social implications. *J. soc. Research*, 1936, 3, 488-493.
16. LEWIN, K. Vorsatz, Wille und Bedürfnis. *Psychol. Forsch.*, 1926, 7, 330-385.
17. LEWIN, K. *Principles of topological psychology*. New York and London: McGraw-Hill, 1936.
18. MALLER, J. B. Cooperation and competition. *Teach. Coll. Contr. Educ.*, 1929, No. 384.
19. MURPHY, G. Address at Symposium: The role of the psychologist in the establishment of better human relations. Meeting of Amer. Psychol. Assn., Boston, Sept. 7, 1948.
20. REICHENBACH, H. *Relativitätstheorie und Erkenntnis a priori*. Berlin: Springer, 1920.
21. Ross, E. A. *Social psychology*. New York: Macmillan, 1908.
22. SHERIF, M. *An outline of social psychology*. New York: Harper, 1948.
23. SIMS, V. M. The relative influence of two types of motivation on improvement. *J. educ. Psychol.*, 1928, 19, 480-484.
24. SKINNER, B. F. *The behavior of organisms*. New York: Appleton-Century-Crofts, 1938.
25. SNYGG, D., and COMBS, A. W. *Individual behavior*. New York: Harper, 1949.
26. TOLMAN, E. C. Cognitive maps in rats and men. *Psychol. Rev.*, 1948, 55, 189-208.
27. VAUGHN, W. F., *Social psychology*. New York: Odyssey Press, 1948.
28. WATSON, J. B. *Psychological care of infant and child*. New York: Norton, 1928.
29. WERTHEIMER, M. Unpublished lectures.
30. WHITEHEAD, T. N. *The industrial worker*. Cambridge, Mass.: Harvard Univ. Press, 1938. Vol. 1.
31. YOUNG, K. *Social psychology*. New York: Crofts, 1944.
32. Dying miners wrote notes to their families as deadly gas crept on them in Illinois pit (Anon.). *New York Times*, March 31, 1947, p. 8.

OVERVIEW

INDIVIDUAL THRESHOLD
FOR PANIC BEHAVIOR

Duane P. Schultz

Brown (1954) suggested that the Mintz analysis suffers from the same shortcomings as other theoretical approaches which invoke the concept of contagion, facilitation, or imitation. They explain how the behavior spreads through a crowd but fail to explain how the behavior originates, initially, in a few members of the crowd. Accordingly, Brown calls for research on the nature of panic-proneness and suggests that there are individual thresholds for this behavior, with some people being more "resistant" to panic behavior than others, as a function of basic personality differences.

It is suggested that research on panic-proneness might proceed from a more physiological basis, that is, in terms of the concept of the level of arousal, as it relates to the individual's "threshold" or optimal level of stimulation. Various investigators have discussed this concept under different terminology: for example, "energy mobilization" (Cannon, 1929; Duffy, 1951), "degree of arousal" (Freeman, 1948), "activation" (Lindsley, 1951), and "level of arousal" (Bindra, 1959).* They all refer to a dimension representing the energy level or excitation level of the organism. At one

---

* W. Cannon, *Bodily changes in pain, hunger, fear, and rage,* New York: Appleton-Century, 1929; E. Duffy, The concept of energy mobilization, *Psychological Review,* 1951, **58**, 30-40; G. Freeman, *The energetics of human behavior,* Ithaca, N.Y.: Cornell Univ. Press, 1948; D. Lindsley, Emotion, in S. Stevens (Ed.), *Handbook of experimental psychology,* New York: Wiley, 1951, pp. 473-516; D. Bindra, *Motivation,* New York: Ronald Press, 1959.

end of this arousal continuum is deep sleep or anesthesia, while at the other is the degree of excitation represented in an epileptic seizure or in panic (Bindra, 1959).

It is not intended to develop here a systematic theory of panic based on level of arousal, but merely to suggest the potential importance of this variable, particularly in the early phase of panic where only a few group members display nonadaptive behavior.

Bindra (1959) discusses the autonomic, somatic, and neural changes that take place within the organism under different levels of stimulation, and notes that there are marked individual differences in both the base level and the degree of reactivity of these physiological functions. Additional findings (Hall, 1938; Fuller, 1951; Bindra and Thompson, 1953)* suggest that these individual differences are determined in part by constitutional factors.

Bindra suggests that there exists an optimal level of arousal for the organism at which behavior is most efficient. The higher the increase in this level of arousal (or the lower the level of arousal), the less efficient becomes the behavior. Perhaps, then, in an unorganized group in a theater fire there exists different thresholds of sensory stimulation for the individual members of the audience. When the visual, auditory, and tactual stimulation—such as sight of smoke, higher noise level, and jostling with neighbors —surpasses this "threshold" level, the individual is no longer capable of efficiently coping with the situation and displays some form of nonrational behavior.

---

* C. Hall, The inheritance of emotionality, *Sigma Xi Quarterly*, 1938, **26**, 17-27; J. Fuller, Genetic variability in some physiological constants of dogs, *American Journal of Physiology*, 1951, **166**, 20-24; D. Bindra and W. Thompson, An evaluation of defecation and urination as measures of fearfulness, *Journal of Comparative and Physiological Psychology*, 1953, **46**, 43-45.

What of a military group which is specifically trained to withstand or cope with a very high degree of sensory stimulation? Bindra suggests that increased practice at performing an activity, with its concomitant increased habit strength of response, will increase the optimal level of stimulation. Hence, the organism is able to perform effectively under a higher level of stimulation. True, the level of stimulation in combat may be greater than that experienced during training, but some evidence suggests that a small increase in the level of arousal, above the level at which an activity has been well practiced, may result in a higher or more efficient level of performance (Siegel and Siegel, 1949; Siegel and Brantley, 1951)*—which may explain why a military unit is able to function with an intense increase in the level of arousal. However, certain of the background or antecedent factors suggested by Foreman (1953) and by Schultz (1964) may operate to weaken men constitutionally and so lower their "threshold." Hence they may no longer be able to tolerate a particular level of stimulation after a number of days of continuous combat with little sleep or food.

Yet as Bindra suggests, these conjectures, due to the paucity of research to support them, are tenuous.

Naturalistic observations of men in combat indicate that they often show marked inefficiency which almost always results from the marked changes in arousal level brought about by the combat situation. White (1956)†, making use of observations by Mira

* P. Siegel and H. Siegel, The effect of emotionality on the water intake of the rat, Journal of Comparative and Physiological Psychology, 1949, **42**, 12-16; P. Siegel and J. Brantley, The relationship of emotionality to the consummatory response of eating, Journal of Experimental Psychology, 1951, **42**, 304-306.

† R. White, The Abnormal Personality, New York: Ronald Press, 1956, 2nd ed.

(1943), discusses the complete disorganization of behavior which sometimes occurs in combat.

As danger mounts, control becomes increasingly difficult. The person's mind begins to be occupied incessantly with the danger. He can no longer inhibit the bodily signs of anxiety; perspiration, tremor, restlessness, fast-beating heart, quickened breathing force themselves upon him. Thought and judgment deteriorate, actions are erratic and poorly controlled, new acts are started before old ones are completed. As he finds it impossible to pull himself together, the person experiences an extremely unpleasant sensation of losing his mental balance' (Mira). Danger seems to be everywhere. When panic begins to reign, the conscious state resembles a nightmare, 'consisting of a peculiar, irregular stream of delirious, distorted mental images, most of which are forgotten when the subject returns to normal.' Scarcely aware of what he is doing, the panic-stricken person may rush wildly about, laughing, shouting, crying in rapid succession (White, 1956, pp. 207-208).

Bindra notes that: "Similar observations, showing a disorganization of the various activities that exist in the repertoire of an individual, have been made in noncombat civilian disasters" (1959, p. 244).

Caldwell, Ranson, and Sacks (1951) discuss the role of strong sensory stimuli and heightened excitement as a contributory factor in panic behavior. They note that as far back as the Gallic War, Caesar's enemies utilized intense auditory stimuli to create panic and confusion among his legions. In more modern warfare, we have examples of the Japanese in World War II, and the North Koreans and Chinese Communists in the Korean conflict, doing the same.

VI

Panic in Nuclear Attack

DISCUSSION

THE POSSIBILITIES OF PANIC IN MASS NUCLEAR ATTACK

In the awesome event of a full-scale nuclear attack on this country, the question as to whether substantial numbers of our population will engage in the behavior we have described as panic has been the subject of much speculation since the end of World War II. Most of the data for these speculations have come from analyses of the atomic bombings of Japan, of the conventional bombings of England and Germany, and of peacetime disasters in this and other countries. In the literature one can find arguments to support both sides of the question of the possibility that a nation-wide panic might occur.

The starting point for our discussion in this chapter is the assumption of a large-scale nuclear attack on the major metropolitan areas of the United States, coming with very little advance warning. It is further assumed that the total attack occurs over a time period f no more than several hours, and that no civil defense preparations other than those existing in early 961 will have been made. To provide an indication f the destruction that would ensue at a local level, 'eter Nordlie and Robert Popper describe, in the list hat follows, the results of an assumed attack on a ity of one and one-half million people hit by two o-megaton airbursts about one mile apart, but generally over the urban center.

1. Multi-story, massive, wall-bearing buildings: severely damaged up to 3½ miles; light damage up to o miles from ground zero.

2. Multi-story buildings with reinforced concrete rame and walls and small window area: severely lamaged up to 7 miles, and lightly damaged up to o miles from ground zero.

3. Telephone and power lines (above ground): otally destroyed up to approximately 13 miles from round zero; little damage beyond that point.

4. Motorized vehicles (cars, buses, trucks, emergency vehicles, etc.): severely damaged up to approxnately 6 miles from ground zero.

5. Highway and railroad truss bridges: collapsed up o 6 miles from ground zero.

6. Streets and highways: probably filled with rubble thus preventing traffic even at points where vehicles night have remained operable) up to 10 miles (approximately) from ground zero.

7. Homes: severely damaged within a 12-mile radius of ground zero.

8. Bridges: destroyed within a 4-mile radius of round zero.

9. Trees will be blown over and roads will be locked within a radius of 6 miles from ground zero.

10. Third-degree burns would be produced on ex-

posed skin up to 20 miles, second-degree burns up t•
25 miles, and first-degree burns up to 41 miles from
ground zero.

11. Radiation dosage would have a lethal effect on
unshielded persons 2.2 miles from ground zero (th
blast and heat from the fireball also would be lethal in
this area).

12. People in ordinary shelters such as basement
within a radius of about 6 to 8 miles from ground zer•
would have to leave the area within 48 hours to kee]
from accumulating a lethal radiation dosage.

13. Death from accumulated radiation is likely fc
people in ordinary basement shelters up to about 1
miles from ground zero.

14. Of the total one and one-half million populatio•
in the hypothetical urban area, over one million ar
likely to be dead or dying after the first two week:
Of the remaining one-half million, over 200,000 woul
probably be injured. (Nordlie and Popper, 1961, p]
9-10. Source materials did not specify time of day c
day of year. It is assumed that these figures are ap
proximate averages.)

And all of this in an instant! What happens next
How will these people behave in the immediate pos
attack period? Will they flee in wild uncontrolle
(and uncontrollable) terror to outlying areas, killin₂
looting, pillaging along the way? Or will they engag
in essentially adaptive behavior: helping the woundec
organizing and participating in rescue operation
obeying those in authority, helping to rebuild the
society? It is to these questions that this chapter
addressed.

Despite the exceedingly high numbers of casualtie
there will undoubtedly be many survivors in all se•
tions of the country, in addition to intact materia

and resources. How rapidly society may rebuild itself (assuming it attempts to do so) would seem to depend largely on the individual and social (collective) behavior in the post-attack period.

Quarantelli (1960) has noted that much of our civil defense planning is based on the assumption that escape behavior of a highly maladaptive, unthinking, and contagious nature will be inevitable in a nuclear attack. Further, he states, the major control problem is considered to be precisely one of stopping this mass flight behavior. And indeed this does seem to be the focus of much of the literature distributed by state and local Civil Defense agencies and was highlighted in an article by Val Peterson (Federal Civil Defense Administrator appointed by former President Eisenhower), written for popular consumption (*Collier's*, 1953). Peterson stated that, "Ninety per cent of all emergency measures after an atomic blast will depend on the prevention of panic among the survivors in the first 90 seconds" (p. 100). He went on to suggest that panic, and not the destruction caused by the bombing, might be the ultimate weapon.

> The consequences of an uncontrolled mass stampede from such a population center as Manhattan are almost incalculable. Even if the four underwater traffic tunnels and the six major bridges leading from the island were left undamaged by an attack, disorganized traffic could soon bottle many of the avenues of escape. Those who did succeed in fleeing the island would pour into adjacent areas to become a hungry, pillaging mob—disrupting disaster relief, overwhelming local police and spreading panic in a widening arc p. 101).

Further to convince the magazine-reading public that they had better start running now, Peterson stated that it is a *fact* that people in this country are the

most panic-prone. But so that not every reader would
immediately drop his magazine and run, he offered
a short self-administered test entitled, "How Panic-
Proof Are You?" (Apparently, those who scored high
on this test could finish reading the magazine safe in
the knowledge that they would not clog up the streets
when the bomb falls.)

In 1954, in an article for the *Bulletin of the Atomic
Scientists*, Philip Wylie wrote that the American public would undoubtedly panic under nuclear attack—
a viewpoint he expressed dramatically in his novel,
Tomorrow! (1954b). Wylie believes that the public
already exhibits hysterical symptoms on a massive
scale which are the result of a deeply repressed fear,
and that this fear and hysteria would be triggered by
a nuclear attack and manifested by the survivors in
panic flight.

> When I reflect that, after a test shot one morning in
> Nevada, the wind changed and the surging dust en-
> veloped us where we stood, numbers of men broke and
> ran though the Rad-Safe crews reported the fallout to
> be harmless—and when I reflect that those men were
> concerned intimately with the bomb and among them
> was high brass from every service branch—I feel cer-
> tain that the public, radiation-scared and terribly ig-
> norant—will run like mad until it drops, *even from the
> dust* (1954a, p. 40).

As though emotional predispositions to panic which
Wylie describes were not enough, he also feels that
certain of the Civil Defense measures will only add
to the catastrophe—particularly the closing of major
roads and highways to all but Civil Defense and military vehicles.

> To think that people, a bomb cloud above, a fire
> storm behind, screaming wounded around and rolling

radioactive dust on their heels, will obey these signs—
is almost insane. . . .

Even if the grownup, normal population obeyed,
there are myriads in every city who could not. More
than a quarter of us are children. About a tenth of our
adults are "emotionally unstable" even without external
provocation. About 6 per cent of every big city population is criminal. Half the hospital beds are occupied by
the mentally ill. In every city, thousands cannot read
English. The bomb would turn them all loose (1954a,
p. 40).

Thus far we have concerned ourselves with only
the proposition that mass panic will inevitably occur,
a view seemingly based on little empirical data, and
espoused primarily by those with little or no profes-
sional training in the social sciences. Social scientists
who have studied the problem express the opposite
view—that is, that any panic which would result from
a large-scale disaster will be localized and not widespread. This conclusion is derived from careful study
of disaster situations and World War II conventional
and atomic bombings. Quarantelli (1960) stated that,
Scientific studies of disasters do not bear out the
existence of pandemonium and chaos, or the extensive
panic-stricken reactions frequently reported in jour-
nalistic and popular accounts, or by involved observers
e.g., relief personnel)" (p. 71). He noted that after
intensive study of disasters, he could find not one
instance where more than three- or four-score people
were involved, including the oft-cited *Invasion from
Mars* broadcast.

In the article which follows, Janis, Chapman, Gillin,
and Spiegel express a similar view.

THE PROBLEM OF PANIC

Irving L. Janis, Dwight W. Chapman,
John P. Gillin, and John P. Spiegel

Panic is undoubtedly a dramatic term, but it is an ambiguous one. It has been used to refer to so many different kinds of behavior—ranging from a wild outburst of flight to paralysis of action—that its meaning has become vague. Often the word is employed merely as a vivid term to refer to any kind of behavior that occurs when people feel afraid or worried. To give the word a specific meaning, it is desirable to apply it to highly emotional behavior which is excited by the presence of an immediate severe threat, and *which results in increasing the danger for the self and for others rather than in reducing it.* This concept of panic recognizes the negative connotation that the term usually carries. Thus, we avoid referring to all instances of excited behavior as panic. In these terms for example, flight is not necessarily panic, for flight may result in *reducing* the danger.

The current hunches and guesses seem to go far beyond the known facts in emphasizing the likelihood of its occurrence in this country. Many of the forecasts and discussions concerning panic which have received wide publicity assume that it will not be too difficult for an enemy nation to strike terror into the hearts of

A statement prepared at the request of the Federal Civil Defense Administration by a subcommittee of the Committee on Disaster Studies, National Research Council, National Academy of Sciences. Reprinted by permission of the Office of Civil Defense, Department of Defense (TB-19-2, June 1955).

Americans—especially through the use of atomic and thermonuclear bombs. To the enormous loss of life and property—so runs the theme—panic or mass hysteria will add devastating disorganization and paralysis, a weapon more horrible in its effects than any known to man.

Mass Panic Occurs Rarely

An assessment of the facts shows that the existing evidence falls far short of supporting such a vivid and dramatic prediction. The authenticated instances of mass panic known to have occurred in the last 50 years have been few in number and have been very restricted in their effect. Although there has been war somewhere in the world almost continuously during this time, it is a significant and somewhat astonishing fact that there have been few instances of mass panic directly connected with enemy attack on a civilian population. Moreover, studies of terrified people who have been stunned by an overwhelming disaster indicate that panic states are usually of short duration, and that excited and irrational behavior can usually be prevented or quickly brought to a stop if effective leadership and realistic information is provided. A striking finding that emerges from observations in large-scale disasters, including the A-bomb attack against Japan and the massive bombing assaults against England and Germany, is that the people who are most frightened and most upset very soon become extremely docile and can easily be induced to conform to the rules and regulations of the local authorities.

The logical conclusion from the evidence, then, is that mass panic is a rare event which arises only under highly specialized circumstances. We do know something about the conditions which give rise to panic behavior—though not as much as we would like.

There are four main factors which are characteristic of the panic-producing situation.

(1) *Partial entrapment.*—There is only one, or, at best an extremely limited number of escape routes from a situation dominated by (2).

(2) *A perceived threat.*—The threat may be physical, or psychological, or a combination of both, and it is usually regarded as being so imminent that there is no time to do anything except to try to escape.

(3) *Partial or complete breakdown of the escape route.*—The escape route becomes blocked off, or jammed, or it is overlooked.

(4) *Front to rear communication failure.*—The false assumption that the exit is still open leads the people at the rear of the mass to exert strong physical or psychological pressure to advance toward it. It is this *pressure from the rear* that causes those at the front to be smothered, crushed, or trampled. In instances where people are trampled to death, as in the Coconut Grove fire, this is usually the single, most important factor.

When a mass panic occurs, it usually happens that people do not actually see the "escape hatch," whatever its nature may be, but infer its existence from the fact that other people are moving in a specific direction. This inference made by the individual is reinforced by statements of people in the immediate vicinity. None of these communications, however, is based on realistic information about the actual conditions at the "escape hatch." The people at the rear of the mass, especially, are too far away from the exit to be able to obtain accurate information about its actual state. Thus, when the exit becomes blocked or jammed, the people at the rear behave as if it were still open.

There is some evidence to support the conclusion that when people know that the escape route is actually blocked, and that no escape is possible, they are likely to remain fatalistically hopeful or else become apathetic and depressed—but the likelihood of panic behavior is actually very slight.

Planning for Panic Prevention

The relatively simple panic-producing conditions outlined above are subject to administrative modification or control. Planning for defense against A-bomb or H-bomb disaster would include consideration of ways and means of preventing panic in two types of situations.

The first type is the situation after a major disaster has struck, where thousands of injured, confused, or stunned survivors are seeking to escape from fires and from other sources of danger in their immediate area. Here the major problem is posed by the likelihood that large numbers of trapped people will converge upon limited escape routes. Advance planning requires the establishment of a number of alternative escape routes from each target area. Of even greater importance is continual reconnaissance of the flow of people and traffic. This should preferably take place through some method of inspection by air in order to obtain maximum scanning of the affected area, and of the condition of the various "escape hatches." Information thus obtained and the resulting instructions should then be relayed over the length and breadth of the traffic stream by available means of communication. If information to the survivors is kept constantly correct and is based upon reality, the possibility of postdisaster panic will be markedly reduced.

A second type of situation is one which seems to be given exaggerated prominence in publicity about panic, namely that of a community which believes it is threatened by a devastating blow. Here the central problem is to keep people working efficiently at necessary jobs and to prevent activity that may interfere with preparations to meet the disaster. To prepare for such situations, the major panic prevention devices consist essentially of putting the emergency plans for protecting the population into action and calling public attention to the plans. Above all, people need to know what is expected of them. This means that they need to be given clear-cut information as to what the dangers are and how to cope with them. Rather than giving rise to social disorganization, paralysis, or hysteria, accurate information is likely to promote behavior which is directed realistically toward meeting the emergency.

Resourcefulness in Crisis

The impressive fact that emerges from the study of both wartime and peacetime disasters in this country and abroad is that a large proportion of the affected population spontaneously engages in behavior which enables them to cope fairly effectively with the crisis situation. Observers of disaster situations are repeatedly impressed with the resourcefulness of both the individuals and the social organizations within the community. This does not mean that conflict, confusion, and despair do not occur. But, usually this takes place where incomplete information, ambiguity, conflicting messages, and jammed communication circuits exist.

In short, the problem is to enable the natural human resources of this country to function effectively in the event of a national emergency. What is needed is planning which is based on the realities of the expected emergency and which can guide and channel the spontaneous resources, resistance, and energies of the people. Those who predict that a large number of Americans will react to the threat of an enemy attack by becoming panic-stricken are not basing their opinion on the existing evidence. Moreover, to emphasize the likelihood of panic is to promote the suggestion to the American people that this sort of behavior is expected of them. Finally, it distracts the attention of the administrator from more serious problems of a practical nature such as developing plans for emergency evacuation, providing shelters, and preparing for numerous welfare needs. There is every reason to believe that, rather than panic, the dominant reaction of the American people will continue to be an energetic, adaptive response to whatever threats and dangers they face.

OVERVIEW

Duane P. Schultz

The only evidence, then, that is even remotely related to a nuclear attack situation forces one to the logical conclusion that there will not be mass panic behavior in the event of a nationwide nuclear attack. That there are gross differences in intensity and magnitude between the nuclear attack described earlier and the peacetime disasters and World War II bombings cannot, of course, be denied, although they have often been overlooked. Our discussion, then, must include a consideration of some of the major and more obvious points of difference which may operate to decrease the validity of the generalizations which have been made.

In the first place, with regard to natural disasters and the Japanese atomic bombings, there was restriction of the area of impact. The geographical area affected was localized and nowhere near nationwide proportions. The importance of this point is that the larger area of society remained intact and was ready and able to send rapid assistance. Witness the prompt convergence of Red Cross and military units to disaster scenes all over the world, quickly providing medical care, food, clothing, and shelter for the survivors. In addition, these outside agencies also act as substitutes for the destroyed social structure and organization. But in a nationwide nuclear attack, who will be able to provide social structure, or food? With thousands upon thousands of wounded, dazed, and confused survivors streaming from the attacked cities what organizations will be equipped to aid them? Add to these survivors thousands of others who may leave undamaged cities in fear of an attack, and we have a situation which would be difficult to control—assuming that the authority and mechanisms of control are still extant.

A second point of difference relates to those who survive the initial shock of a disaster. In the case of natural catastrophes, a person surviving an earthquake or a flood no longer need fear for his physical survival: he has lived through the worst. Such a feeling was apparently operative, at first, among the Hiroshima and Nagasaki residents who survived the initial blast and fire. They were completely unaware of any possible lingering deadly effects of fallout. Indeed many Japanese survivors returned to the cities in short order, feeling safe, after having survived the initial blast. The American public, however, has been exposed to informational campaigns about fallout. They know that it is not enough merely to survive the blast—they know they must quickly get miles away from ground zero. The public today has some idea of what to expect and what to fear which the victims of the Japanese attack did not.

Finally, survivors of a nuclear holocaust may be left with the stunning realization (or at least expectation) that their own society, and perhaps that of all nations, has suffered a disastrous blow. The incident of a disaster simultaneously experienced by most of the earth's population would be a unique occurrence in human history. True, there have been instances of society-wide disasters, such as the Black Death, from which the society has eventually recovered, but these disasters occurred gradually, over a period of years—not in hours.

Then too, there may exist a pre-nuclear-disaster attitude on the part of the American people quite different from that of other peoples who were faced with wartime conventional bombing raids. Nordlie and Popper (1961), in reviewing the literature on nuclear war reported that the most frequently encountered remark is, "If the bombs start falling, I hope I get hit immediately; I don't want to survive" (p. 21). This feeling is in marked contrast to the very high morale reported among the British civilian population in the face of constant bombings during the early years of World War II. How widely held is this belief and how it might be reflected in post-attack behavior is not known, but it would seem to represent a potentially important factor in morale.

The author is currently engaged in a large-sample survey of the opinions of college students on the use of nuclear weapons and on their expectations of behavior in a nuclear attack. Based on the hypothesis that behavior in a certain situation may be partly determined by how people anticipate that they and others will behave, subjects are asked to indicate what they think the behavior of the American people will be in a nuclear attack. Subjects are presented with a scale ranging from a completely helpless and confused state of behavior, through behavior characterized by much mutual aid and cooperation, to completely irrational, amoral, and chaotic behavior where all semblance of society is lost. With a sample of only 150 subjects (out of an eventual 1,000), 16 per cent feel that "panic behavior" will occur in case of nuclear attack. However, when the data are broken down into two groups of younger (freshman-sophomore) versus older (junior-senior) students, we find a striking difference in their predilections. Thus while 25 per cent of the older students feel that panic behavior would result, only 10 per cent of the younger ones checked this alternative. Sixty-eight per cent of the younger students feel that the behavior would be that of mutual aid and cooperation, compared with only 28 per cent of the older students. The data, let us emphasize, are not complete nor have the reasons for the students' choices as yet been analyzed, but even what we do have suggests an interesting developmental trend. This study will be extended to include groups of high school and post-college age students. Certainly there are many facets of the problem of pre-disaster attitudes which remain for investigation.

So far, we can draw inferences only from that data which already exists, since fortunately, there have been no large-scale nuclear attacks which could provide further information. But even the available evidence we do have does not provide sufficient basis on which to predict that survivors of a nuclear attack would behave in ways significantly different from survivors of past disasters. In the absence of evidence to the contrary, we are left with the historical truth that throughout man's history, societies have sustained overwhelming natural and man-made disasters from which they have recovered—to some level of efficiency.

Bibliography

This selected list of references is an elaboration of the bibliography on panic contained in *The Problem of Panic* (Federal Civil Defense Administration Technical Bulletin, TB-19-2, 1955). Forty-five recent articles in the area have been added.

Air raids, discipline and panic. *Lancet,* 1938, 1, 1061.

ALLPORT, F. *Social psychology.* Boston: Houghton Mifflin, 1924.

American National Red Cross. *Coconut Grove Fire.* Washington: Am. Nat. Red Cross, 1943, ARC 1510.

American National Red Cross. *Hartford Circus Fire.* Washington: Am. Nat. Red Cross, 1946, ARC 1525.

An eye-witness of the 'gas-battle' at Ypres. *Literary Digest,* 1915, 51, 483-486.

An introduction to the psychiatric aspects of civil defense. Topeka: Group for the Advancement of Psychiatry, 1951.

Anatomy of panic; review of the "Invasion from Mars." *Time,* April 15, 1940, 35, 58-60.

ANDREWS, L. *Military manpower.* New York: Dutton, 1920.

ANGLE, P. (Ed.) *The great Chicago Fire.* Chicago: Chicago Historical Society, 1946.

Anti-panic. *Spectator,* 1893, 71, 869-870.

ARMSTRONG-JONES, R. The psychology of fear and the effects of panic fear in war time. *Journal of Mental Science,* 1917, 63, 346-389.

AVELING, F. Notes on the emotion of fear as observed in conditions of warfare. *British Journal of Psychology,* 1929, 20, 137-144.

BAARSLAG, K. *SOS to the rescue.* New York: Oxford, 1940.

BAKER, G. and CHAPMAN, D. *Man and society in disaster*. New York: Basic Books, 1962.

BALDWIN, H. *Admiral Death*. New York: Simon and Schuster, 1938.

BANNER, H. *Calamities of the world*. London: Hurst and Blackett Ltd., 1932.

BANNER, H. *Great disasters of the world*. London: Hurst and Blackett Ltd., 1931.

BARRETT, J. When cholera came. *McClure*, 1900, **16**, 140-144.

BARTLETT, R. The civilian population under bombardment. *Nature*, 1941, **147**, 700-701.

BATTEN, M. Memories of a great forest fire. *Blackwood*, 1941, **250**, 47-57.

BEESLEY, L. *The loss of the Titanic*. London: Philip Allan, 1929.

BELDEN, J. *Still time to die*. New York: Harper, 1944.

BERRY, C. *Loss of the Sultana and reminiscences of survivors*. Lansing, Michigan: Darius Thorp, 1892.

BETZ, B. Psychological effects of atomic warfare. Address at Johns Hopkins University School of Public Health, April 1, 1950. See *The Evening Sun* (Baltimore) and *The Sun* (Baltimore) same date.

BINNS, J. How people behave when in danger. *American Magazine*, 1920, **90**, 26-28, 90, 93-94, 97-98.

BIRCHER, E. Panic: nature, causes and treatment. *Schweizerische Medizinische Wochenschrift*, 1939, **69**, 768ff.

BIRD, C. *Social psychology*. New York: Appleton-Century, 1940.

BORING, E., LANGFELD, H., and WELD, H. *Foundations of psychology*. New York: Wiley, 1948.

BORING, E. (Ed.) *Psychology for the Armed Forces*. Washington: The Infantry Journal, 1945.

BRINKMAN, D. Neue Gesichspunkte Zur Psychologie der Panik. *Schweizer Zur Psychologie Anwend*, 1944, **3**, 3-15.

BROSIN, H. Panic states and their treatment. *American Journal of Psychiatry*, 1943, **100**, 54-61.

BROUSSEAU, A. *Essai sur la peur aux armées, 1914-1918*. Paris: Felix Alcan, 1920.

BROWN, R. Mass phenomena. In G. Lindzey (Ed.), *Handbook of social psychology*. Reading, Mass.: Addison-Wesley, 1954, Chapter 23.

BULL, N. The dual character of fear. *Journal of Psychology*, 1938, **5**, 209-218.

BUSCH, P. Flight. *National Review*, 1948, **131**, 150-152.

CALDWELL, J., RANSON, S., and SACKS, J. Group panic and other mass disruptive reactions. *U.S. Armed Forces Medical Journal*, 1951, **2**, 541-567.

California, Office of Civil Defense. *Panic control and prevention: instructor's manual and teaching outline.* Sacramento: Office of Civil Defense, 1951.

CAMERON, N. *The psychology of behavior disorders.* New York: Houghton Mifflin, 1947.

CANTRIL, H. Causes and control of riot and panic. *Public Opinion Quarterly,* 1943, 7, 669-679.

CANTRIL, H. *The invasion from Mars.* Princeton: Princeton University Press, 1940.

CARR, M. Drought. *Blackwood,* 1948, 260, 150-152.

Catastrophe. *Time,* December, 1942, 40, 43-44.

CATTELL, R. *General psychology.* Cambridge: Sci-Art, 1941.

CHAPMAN, D. (Ed.) Human behavior in disaster: a new field of social research. *Journal of Social Issues,* 1954, 10.

Cholera panic. *Spectator,* 1892, 63, 58-59.

CHURCHILL, E. Panic in disaster. *Annals Surgery,* 1953, 138, 935-936.

Civil Defense and Disaster Committee. *The origin and nature of panic.* Milwaukee: CD and Disaster Committee, 1951.

CLIFFORD, H. In the days of the chilly death. *Living Age,* 1901, 231, 26-34.

COBLENTZ, S. Earthquake, fire and flood (in the eyes of childhood). *Pacific Spectator,* 1950, 4, 144-152.

COLBERT, E. and CHAMBERLIN, E. Chicago and the great conflagration. Cincinnati: Vent, 1871.

The Collected Papers of Wilfred Trotter. London: Oxford, 1941.

COLLMAN, C. *Our mysterious panics 1830-1930.* New York: Morrow, 1931.

Controlled anxiety aim of civil defense. *Safety Review,* 1951, (May), 7-8.

COONEY, J. Army doctors say mass hysteria need not follow atomic bomb explosion. *Military Surgeon,* 1948, 102, 501-503.

COONEY, J. Psychological factors in atomic warfare. U.S. Armed Forces Special Weapons Project, Radiological Defense, Volume 3. Washington: U.S. Govt. Printing Office, 1950.

COSTE, C. *La psychologie du combat.* Paris: Berger-Levrault, 1929.

COULTON, G. *The black death.* New York: McBride, 1930.

CRAWFORD, M. Greatest disaster of history (Italian quake of 1906). *Outlook,* 1909, 91, 673-690.

CROWTHER, S. An old fashioned banker: memories of booms and panics. *Saturday Evening Post,* 1932, 205, 4-5.

CSOKOR, F. *A civilian in the Polish War.* London: Secker and Warburg, 1940.

CYGIELSTREJCH, A. La psychologie de la panique pendant la guerre. *Annales Medico-Psychologiques,* 1916, 7, 172-192.

DAVIES, J. Air-raid: the technique of silent approach. London: Routledge, 1938.

DEMERATH, N. and WALLACE, A. (Eds.) Human adaptation to disaster. *Human Organization,* 1957, 16.

DIETHELM, O. Panic. *Archives of Neurology and Psychiatry,* 1932, 28, 1153-1168.

DIETHELM, O. Nosological position of panic reactions. *American Journal of Psychiatry,* 1934, 13, 1295-1316.

DOCKERAY, F. *Psychology.* New York: Prentice-Hall, 1942.

DOLLARD, J. *Fear in battle.* New Haven: Institute of Human Relations, 1943.

DRINKER, F. *Horrors of tornado, flood and fire.* Harrisburg, Pennsylvania: Minter, 1913.

DUDYCHA, G. *Applied psychology.* New York: Ronald Press, 1963.

The Earthquake Seen Through Japanese Eyes. *Literary Digest,* 1923, 79, 39-44.

ELTLINGE, L. *The psychology of war.* Fort Leavenworth: Press of the Army Service School, 1917.

Encyclopedia Britannica. Panic. Volume 17, 17th edition.

Eos. My earthquake experience. *Blackwood,* 1934, 235, 20-32.

ERICKSON, H., NYSWANDER, D., ZIMMERMAN, K., and SKEELS, H. *Mental health implications in civilian emergencies.* Report of Subcommittee on Civil Defense, Community Service Committee, National Advisory Mental Health Council, U.S. Dept. of Health, Education, and Welfare, May, 1953.

ERLEIGHT, V. *The South Sea bubble.* New York: Putnam, 1933.

FALLA, W. Fear factors in flying personnel. *Journal of Mental Science,* 1947, 93, 43-54.

FARAGO, L. *German psychological warfare.* New York: Putnam, 1942.

FARROW, E. Panic. *Farrow's Military Encyclopedia,* Vol. II, 1895.

Federal Civil Defense Administration Technical Bulletin, TB-7-1. *The role of the warden in panic prevention.* September, 1956.

FOGLEMAN, C. and PARENTON, V. Disaster and aftermath: selected aspects of individual and group behavior in critical situations. *Social Forces,* 1959, 38, 129-135.

FOREMAN, P. Panic theory. *Sociology and Social Research,* 1953, 37, 295-304.

FRANCES, D. Refugees. *Blackwood*, 1940, 248, 354-367.

FRANTL, K. *First-aid treatment of psychiatric casualties*. Los Angeles City Civil Defense and Disaster Corps Division Health Service Outline for Training Personnel. The Insurance Index, Volume XIII, No. 19 (December) 1951.

FREEMAN, D. and COOPER, D. *The road to Bordeaux*. London: Cresset, 1940.

FREIWALD, L. *Last days of the German fleet*. London: Constable, 1932.

FRENCH, J. Experimental study of group panic. *Journal of the Elisha Mitchell Scientific Society*, 1941, 57, 195.

FRENCH, J. Organized and unorganized groups under fear and frustration. *University of Iowa Studies: Studies in Child Welfare*. Iowa City: University of Iowa Press, 1944.

FREUD, S. *Group psychology and the analysis of the ego*. London: Hogarth Press, 1922.

FREY, T. Psychological preparedness for war and possibilities of controlling panic. *Svenska Lakartidningen*, June 15, 1951, 48, 1465-1478.

FRIBOURG-BLANC. La panique aux armées. *La Presse Medicale*, 1938, 46, 521-523.

FRITZ, C. Disaster. In R. Merton and R. Nisbet, *Contemporary social problems*. New York: Harcourt Brace, 1961, pp. 651-694.

FRITZ, C. and MATHEWSON, J. *Convergence behavior in disasters: a problem in social control*. Washington: Committee on Disaster Studies, 1957.

FRITZ, C. and WILLIAMS, H. The human being in disasters: a research perspective. *Annals American Academy of Political and Social Science*, 1957, 309, 42-51.

GALDSTON, I. (Ed.) *Panic and morale*. New York: Academy of Medicine, 1958.

GARDNER, C. Assemblies. *American Journal of Sociology*, 1914, 19, 531-555.

GIBSON, J. Fear: most contagious disease. *Science Digest*, July 1951, 30, 67-71.

GODBEY, A. *Great disasters and horrors in the world's history*. St. Louis: Excelsior, 1890.

GOLDSTEIN, R. Problems in emergency practice; mental casualties. *Connecticut Medical Society*, 1942, 6, 522-527.

GREENE, J. (Ed.) *The infantry journal reader*. New York: Doubleday, 1943.

GREENWOOD. Panic in wartime. *British Medical Journal*, 1940, 1, 448.

GRINKER, R. and SPIEGEL, J. *Men under stress*. Philadelphia: Blakiston, 1945.

HADFIELD, R. *Sea-toll of our time.* London: Witherby, 1930.

HALSTEAD, M. *Galveston: the horrors of a stricken city.* American Publishers' Association, 1900.

HARTENBERG, P. Les émotions de bourse: notes des psychologie collective. *Revue Philosophique,* 1904, **58**, 162-170.

HIRSHLEIFER, J. Some thoughts on the social structure after a bombing disaster. *World Politics,* 1956, **8**, 206-227.

HOOD, A. Personal experiences of the great earthquake. *Living Age,* 1909, **261**, 355-365.

HOOK, J. Buried alive. *Harper,* 1928, **157**, 483-491.

HOWLAND, S. *Steamboat disasters and railroad accidents in the U.S.* Worcester: Dorr, Howland, 1840.

IDLE, E. *War over West Ham.* London: Faber and Faber, 1943.

IKLE, F. *The social impact of bomb destruction.* Norman: University of Oklahoma Press, 1958.

IKLE, F., QUARANTELLI, E., RAYNER, J., and WITHEY, S. *Withdrawal behavior in disasters: escape, flight and evacuation.* Washington: Committee on Disaster Studies, 1958.

Information and training for civil defense. Part IX of the Report of Project East River. New York: Associated Universities, 1952.

JANIS, I. *Air war and emotional stress.* New York: McGraw-Hill, 1951.

JANIS, I. *The psychological impact of air attacks: a survey and analysis of observation on civilian reactions during World War II.* Washington: Rand Corporation, 1949.

JANIS, I., CHAPMAN, D., GILLIN, J., and SPIEGEL, J. *The problem of panic.* Washington: Federal Civil Defense Administration, 1955, TB-19-2.

JOHNSON, L. *Floodtide of 1927.* Randolph, Vermont: Johnson, 1927.

JOHNSTON, R. *Bull Run: its strategy and tactics.* Boston: Houghton Mifflin, 1913.

KARTMAN, B. and BROWN, L. (Eds.) *Disaster!* New York: Pellegrini and Cudahy, 1948.

KELLAND, C. Panic: how men and women act when facing terror. *The American Magazine,* 1930, **109**, 44-45, 92-95.

KOETTGEN, J. *A German deserter's war experience.* New York: Huebsch, 1917.

KROUT, M. *Introduction to social psychology.* New York: Harper, 1942.

LANHAM, C. Panic. *Infantry Journal,* 1937, **44**, 301-308.

LAPIERE, R. *Collective behavior.* New York: McGraw-Hill, 1938.

LAURIAT, C. *The Lusitania's last voyage.* Boston: Houghton Mifflin, 1915.

LEBON, G. *The crowd.* London: Ernest Benn Ltd., 1896.

LEFLER, H. My sixty sleepless hours. *McClure*, 1906, 27, 275-281.

LEIGHTON, A. and Low, R. *Psychological factors in major disasters.* Rochester: University of Rochester Medical Projects Reports, 1951.

LEMEILLOUR. Etude sur la panique. *Journal de Medicine de Bordeaux*, 1920, 91, 598-605.

LINDESMITH, A. and STRAUSS, A. *Social psychology.* New York: Dryden, 1949.

LINEBARGER, P. *Psychological warfare.* Washington: Infantry Journal Press, 1948.

LINTHICUM, R. and WHITE, T. *The complete story of the San Francisco horror.* Chicago: Hubert Russell, 1906.

LOCKHART, J. *Perils of the sea.* New York: Stokes, 1925.

LOEWENBERG, R. Rumors of mass poisoning in times of crisis. *Journal of Criminal Psychopathology*, 1943, 5, 131-142.

LOGAN, L., KILLIAN, L., and MARS, W. *A study of the effects of catastrophe on social disorganization.* Chevy Chase, Maryland: Johns Hopkins University, Operations Research Office, 1952.

LORD, H. *The psychology of courage.* Boston: Luce, 1918.

LYONS, T. Dakota blizzard. *Commonweal*, 1940, 33, 251-253.

MACDONALD, A. General Slocum disaster. *American Mercury*, 1939, 47, 203-208.

MACDONALD, C. Great panics. *North American Review*, 1908, 187, 183-192.

MCDOUGALL, W. *The group mind.* London: Cambridge, 1920.

MCDOUGALL, W. *Social psychology.* Boston: Luce, 1923.

MCNEAL, M. Destruction of Tokyo; impressions of an eyewitness. *Catholic World*, 1923, 118, 306-317.

MARKS, E. *Human reactions in disaster situations.* Unpublished report, National Opinion Research Center, 1954.

MARKS, E. and FRITZ, C. The NORC studies of human behavior in disaster. *Journal of Social Issues*, 1954, 10, 26-31.

MARSHALL, J. Death from the sky; this is what people think and say and do when bombs fall. *Collier's*, 1937, 100, 9-10, 28.

MARSHALL, L. *The sinking of the Titanic and great ship disasters.* L. L. Myers, 1912.

MARSHALL, S. *Men against fire.* New York: Morrow, 1947.

MARSHALL, W. Biological reactions to earthquakes. *Journal of Abnormal and Social Psychology*, 1935-1936, 30, 462-467.

MARTIN, A. Prevention of panic. *Mental Hygiene,* 1942, **26,** 546-553.

MARTIN, P. *Emotional preparation for atomic bombing.* Detroit: Civil Defense and Disaster Committee, Wayne County Medical Society, 1951.

MARTIN, P. A psychiatric viewpoint on civil defense. *Journal of the Michigan Medical Society,* 1951, **50,** 278-281.

MASTERS, D. *SOS: A book of sea adventure.* New York: Holt, 1934.

MATHER, M. I was on the Hindenburg. *Harper,* 1937, **175,** 590-595.

MAXWELL, W. *A psychological retrospect of the great war.* New York: MacMillan, 1923.

MAY, R. *The meaning of anxiety.* New York: MacMillan, 1940.

MEERLOO, J. Delusion and mass delusion. *Nervous and Mental Disease Monographs,* 1949, No. 79.

MEERLOO, J. First aid in acute panic states. *American Journal of Psychotherapy,* 1951, **5,** 367-371.

MEERLOO, J. *Patterns of panic.* New York: International Universities Press, 1950.

MEERLOO, J. Danger, panic, and first-aid. *Military Review of Fort Leavenworth,* 1953, **33,** 40-45.

MEIER, N. *Military psychology.* New York: Harper, 1943.

MENNINGER, W. Psychological reactions in an emergency (flood). *American Journal of Psychiatry,* 1952, **109,** 128-130.

Mental First Aid. *Science News Letter,* 1951, **59,** 53.

MILLER, E. (Ed.) *The neuroses in war.* New York: MacMillan, 1940.

Milwaukee Civil Defense and Disaster Committee. *The origin and nature of panic.* Milwaukee: Public Information and Education Division, June, 1951.

MINTZ, A. Non-adaptive group behavior. *Journal of Abnormal and Social Psychology,* 1951, **46,** 150-159.

MIRA, E. *Psychiatry in war.* New York: Norton, 1943.

MORRIS, C. (Ed.) *Morris's story of the great earthquake of 1908 and other historic disasters.* E. M. Scull, 1909.

MUNN, N. *Psychology.* Boston: Houghton Mifflin, 1946.

MUNSON, E. *The management of men.* New York: Holt, 1921.

My experiences of earthquake. *Eclectic,* 1860, **50,** 212-214.

NAGAI, T. *We of Nagasaki.* New York: Duell, Sloan and Pearce, 1951.

National Opinion Research Center Disaster Project, unpublished interviews.

National Research Council. *Psychology for the fighting man.* Washington: The Infantry Journal, 1943.

NEIL, H. *Chicago's awful theater horror.* Chicago: Memorial Publishing Co., 1904.

NICHOLSON, C. My experiences on a sinking ship. *Overland,* 1915, 66, 329-330.

NOHL, J. *The black death: a chronicle of the plague.* London: Allen and Unwin, 1926.

NORDLIE, P. and POPPER, R. *Social phenomena in a post-nuclear attack situation.* Arlington, Virginia: Human Sciences Research, 1961.

NOYES, A. Commercial panics, past and future. *Atlantic Monthly,* 1906, 98, 433-445.

Office of the Secretary of Defense. *Stop that rumor.* Washington: U.S. Govt. Printing Office, Armed Forces Talk 350.

Panic aid posts urged. *Science News Letter,* 1951, 59, 374.

Panic and panics. *All the Year Round,* 1878, 21, 512-516.

Panic during plague. *Spectator,* 1883, 56, 862.

Panic in the streets. *Lancet,* 1951, 260, 1219.

Panics. *Spectator,* 1888, 61, 1186.

PAOLUCCI, R. The fate of the viribus unitis. *Fortnightly Review,* 1919, 109, 977-988.

PARSON, J. Prisoners of the flood: my memory of the Dayton disaster. *McClure,* 1913, 41, 39-48.

PENNINGTON, L., HOUGHT, R., and CASE, N. *The psychology of military leadership.* New York: Prentice-Hall, 1943.

PERCIN, A. *Le combat.* Paris: Alcan, 1914.

PERCIN, A. *Souvenirs militaires 1870-1914.* Paris: Edition de L'Armée Nouvelle, 1930.

PETERSON, V. Panic, the ultimate weapon? *Collier's,* August 21, 1953.

PEW, W. *Making a soldier.* Boston: Badger, 1917.

PFUELF, E. *Die panik in kriege.* Munich: Smelin, 1908.

POWELL, J. and RAYNER, J. *Progress notes: disaster investigation.* Maryland: Army Chemical Center, 1952.

PRINCE, S. *Catastrophe and social change.* New York: Columbia University Press, 1920.

Psychological first aid in community disasters. American Psychiatric Association Committee on Civil Defense.

Psychological first aid in disasters. *American Journal of Nursing,* 1955, 55, 437.

QUARANTELLI, E. The nature and conditions of panic. *American Journal of Sociology,* 1954, 60, 267-275.

QUARANTELLI, E. The behavior of panic participants. *Sociology and Social Research,* 1957, 41, 187-194.

QUARANTELLI, E. Images of withdrawal behavior in disasters: some basic misconceptions. *Social Problems,* 1960, 8, 68-79.

QUEEN, STUART, and MANN. *Social pathology.* New York, 1925.

REIWALD, P. *De l'esprit des masses.* Paris: Delachaux and Niestle, 1949.

Reminiscences of Chicago during the great fire. Chicago: Donnelley, 1915.

REUTER, E. and HART, C. *Introduction to sociology.* New York: McGraw-Hill, 1933.

REYNAUD, J. La panique. *Concours Medical,* 1952, 74, 1533-1534.

RICKMAN, J. A discursive review of J. Langdon Davies' "Air Raid." *British Journal of Medical Psychology,* 1938, 17, 361-373.

RICKMAN, J. Panic and air-raid precautions. *Lancet,* 1938, 234, 1291-1295.

RIEZLER, K. *Man: mutable and immutable.* Chicago: Regnery, 1950.

RIEZLER, K. The social psychology of fear. *American Journal of Sociology,* 1944, 49, 489-498.

ROE. Flood. *Blackwood,* 1931, 230, 807-809.

RUCH, F. *Psychology and life.* Chicago: Scott, Foresman, 1948.

SARGENT, S. *Social psychology.* New York: Ronald, 1950.

SARTORIOUS. Psychology of panic in war. *The American Review of Reviews,* 1914, 50, 628-629.

SARTORIUS, H. Die psychologie der massen und die panik in kriege. *The Deutsche Revue,* 1914, 39, 102-112.

SCHMIDEBERG, W. The treatment of panic casualty area and clearing station. *Life and Letters Today,* 1939, 23, 162-169.

SCHMOLLER, G. Les phases typiques des crises economiques et leur histoire. *Revue Economique Internationale,* 1904, 1, 125-151.

SCHULTZ, D. Panic in organized collectivities. *Journal of Social Psychology,* 1964(a), 63, 353-359.

SCHULTZ, D. Theories of panic: a review. *Journal of Social Psychology,* 1964(b), *in press.*

SEVAREID, E. Worm's eye-view: when bombs fall, the victims are usually steadfast but their reactions are unpredictable. *Current History and Forum,* 1940, 52, 17-19.

SENIOR, W. *Notable shipwrecks.* London: Cassell, Petter, and Galpin, 1873.

SHAFFER, L. Fear and courage in aerial combat. *Journal of Consulting Psychology,* 1947, 11, 137-143.

SHANAS, E. *The nature and manipulation of crowds.* Chicago: University of Chicago, Department of Sociology, 1937, unpublished MA thesis.

SHASKAN, D. Group therapy and the prevention of panic. *In-*

ternational Journal of Group Psychotherapy, 1953, **3**, 285-292.

SHAW, F. *Famous shipwrecks.* London: Elikin Mathews and Marrot, 1930.

SHERIF, M. *An outline of social psychology.* New York: Harper, 1948.

SHILS, E. and JANOWITZ, M. Cohesion and disintegration in the Wehrmacht in World War II. *Public Opinion Quarterly,* 1948,12, 280-315.

SHOUP, E. How the earthquake felt at San Jose. *The Independent,* 1906, **60**, 1158.

SIEMES, F. Hiroshima, August 6, 1945. *Bulletin of the Atomic Scientists,* 1946, **1**, 2-6.

SIMIAND, F. La psychologie social des crises and les flucturation economique de courte duree. *Annales Sociologiques,* 1937, **2**, 3-32.

SKI. Torpedoed. *Living Age,* 1916, **289**, 734-740.

SLADE, W. Earthquake psychology. *Australasian Journal of Psychology and Philosophy,* 1932, **10**, 58-63.

Soldiers' panics. *Every Saturday,* 1870, **1**, 581.

SMITH, C. (Ed.) *Adventures and perils.* London: Joseph, 1936.

SNOW, E. *Great storms and famous shipwrecks of the New England Coast.* Boston: Yankee, 1943.

SPIEGEL, J. Cry wolf, cry havoc. *Bulletin of the Atomic Scientists,* 1954, **10**, 134-135.

SPURGEON, A. *The burning of the Volturno.* London: Cassell, 1913.

STALKER, H. Panic states in civilians. *British Medical Journal,* 1940, **1**, 887-889.

Stanford Research Institute. *Impact of air attack in World War II.* Selected data for civil defense planning. Division III: Social disorganization, behavior, and morale under stress of bombing. Vol. I: Public attitudes and behavior. Menlo Park, California: Stanford Research Institute, 1953.

STARCK. Paniken. *Beiheft, Z. Militar-Wochenblatt,* 1904, 447-463.

STOVKIS, B. Psychology of the individual and the mass in a state of panic. *Nederlandsch Titdschrift Voor Psychologie,* 1939, **7**, 296-308.

STONE, T. Man, fear, and panic. *Infantry Journal,* 1941, 349.

STOUFFER, S. *The American soldier: combat and its aftermath.* Vol. II. Princeton: Princeton University Press, 1949.

STRAUSS, A. The literature on panic. *Journal of Abnormal and Social Psychology,* 1944, **29**, 317-328.

SULLIVAN, H. The meaning of anxiety in psychiatry and in life. *Psychiatry,* 1948, **11**, 1-15.

SWINTON, W. *The twelve decisive battles of the war.* New York: Dick and Fitzgerald, 1871.

THOMAS, W. *Source book for social origins.* Boston: Gorham, 1909.

THOULESS, R. *Social psychology.* London: University Tutorial Press, 1932.

TITMUS, R. *Problems of social policy.* London: Longmans, Green, 1950.

TORYAKIAN, E. Aftermath of a thermonuclear attack on the United States: some sociological considerations. *Social Problems,* 1959, 6, 291-303.

Transactions of the conference on morale and prevention and control of panic. New York: New York Academy of Medicine and Josiah Macy, Jr. Foundation, 1951.

TROTTER, W. Panic and its consequences. *British Medical Journal,* 1940, 1, 270.

TSUZUKI, M. *Report on the medical studies of effects of the atomic bomb.* Washington: General Report, Atomic Bomb Casualty Commission, National Research Council, 1947.

TURNER, R. and KILLIAN, L. *Collective behavior.* Englewood Cliffs, New Jersey: Prentice-Hall, 1957.

TYHURST, J. *Behaviour under stress.* Ottawa, Canada: Defense Research Board, 1950, No. 19.

U.S. Strategic Bombing Survey, Morale Division. *The effects of strategic bombing on German morale.* Washington: U.S. Govt. Printing Office, 1947, Vol. II.

VANCE, J. (Ed.) *The great floods of 1884 in the Ohio Valley.* Gallipolis, Ohio: The Bulletin Office, 1884.

VAUGHT, E. The release and heightening of individual reactions in crowds. *Journal of Abnormal and Social Psychology,* 1928, 22, 414-415.

VERNON, P. Psychological effects of air-raids. *Journal of Abnormal and Social Psychology,* 1941, 36, 457-476.

VON ALTROCK, C. Panic. *Infantry Journal,* 1930, 37, 116-118.

WAELDER, R. *Psychological aspects of war and peace.* Geneva: Geneva Research Center, 1939.

WAGGONER, R. and HIMLER, L. Psychiatric aspects of civilian defense. *Journal of the Michigan Medical Society,* 1951, 50, 278-281.

WARDLE, M. Notes on fear in war. *Army Quarterly,* 1922, 4, 263-273.

WAUTHIER, M. La peur. *Revue de L'Université de Bruxelles,* 1937-1938, 43, 65-68, 172-196.

WEGIERSKI, D. *September 1939.* London: Minerva, 1940.

WEINSBERG, S. The combat neuroses. *American Journal of Sociology,* 1946, 50, 465-478.

Why some soldiers run away. *Literary Digest,* 1914, 49, 626-627.

WINKLER, E. and ORLICH, W. Zum panik problem. *Soldatentum,* 1937, 4, 291-296.

WYLIE, P. Panic, psychology, and the bomb. *Bulletin of the Atomic Scientists,* 1954, 10, 37-40.

WYLIE, P. *Tomorrow!* New York: Holt, Rinehart and Winston, 1954.

YOUNG, E. Environmental stress and personal adjustment. *Sociology and Social Research,* 1950, 35, 91-96.

YOUNG, K. *Social psychology.* New York: Appleton-Century-Crofts, 1956.

YOUNG, P. *Emotion in man and animal.* New York: Wiley, 1943.

YOUNG, P. Emotion as a disorganized response—a reply to Professor Leeper. *Psychological Review,* 1949, 56, 184-191.

Index